MORE SIMPLY SUPER STORY TIMES

Programming Ideas for Ages 3-6

W9-AGH-482

Marie Castellano Boyum

UpstartBooks

Fort Atkinson, Wisconsin

Dedication—

To all who have children in their lives and know they are a true gift.
May you utilize this book to assist our future generations to
develop a lifelong love of books.

KHB thanks for my gift of belief, respect, and love.

Published by UpstartBooks
W5527 Highway 106
P.O. Box 800
Fort Atkinson, Wisconsin 53538-0800
1-800-448-4887

© Marie Castellano, 2006
Cover design: Debra Neu

The paper used in this publication meets the minimum requirements of American National Standard for Information Science — Permanence of Paper for Printed Library Material. ANSI/NISO Z39.48-1992.

Note: *All efforts have been made to obtain permission for the fingerplays and songs in this book. If the author is not listed, the original author is unknown. We apologize for any omissions.*

Contents

Introduction

My goal is to show anyone who spends time with young children a unique, simple approach to building upon a child's passion for learning. By combining activities with stories, the knowledge children gain from hearing books read aloud can be greatly expanded. As in *Simply Super Storytimes,* my desire with *More Simply Super Storytimes* remains that all children learn a lifelong love of books and reading. Although this book is a companion to the first, it can stand alone as a guide that will assist in enhancing the books you share with children.

Use the crafts and other activities to reinforce the concepts in the various themes of stories. Having a tangible object for children to be proud of helps encourage not only their self-esteem, but it also reinforces narration skills necessary to pre-reading development. Encourage your children to discuss what stories they heard and the projects and activities they did.

If you are working with other people's children, encourage parents to continue with the theme, possibly giving them portions of the chapter to do at home, as well as a list of the books you read. This enables children to enjoy their favorite books again and encourages interaction with the parent and child at home. It also models print motivation, another important pre-reading skill. See page 10 for more information on pre-reading skills.

The more children see how books span so many areas of our lives, the more excited they will be about learning to read themselves. In addition, by using projects to expand on ideas presented in books, you are able to reach more children. Those who have difficulty listening may be interested in other areas, such as math and science, art, or music and movement.

The storytime themes in this book are structured for ages 3–6. You may wish to vary the themes in order to use them with slightly older children. The book list with each chapter is only a guide and you may wish to add or change the themes according to your needs. Some of the books may be out of print, but they are worthy of mention. I apologize in advance if they are difficult to obtain, but remember that libraries are a wonderful resource for all materials. You may also wish to check online for purchasing used and out-of-print materials.

How to Use This Book

This book is divided into themed storytimes. Each theme begins with the same introductory song, which allows the children to feel comfortable knowing what is expected of them. Once they are familiar with the song you may wish to speed up or slow down the tune, as well as change words or actions. Each theme also includes songs, fingerplays, and suggested stories to share. Pick and choose which ideas work best for you, and then intersperse the fingerplays and songs between the stories. Don't like to sing? Try rapping the music by giving it a "boom-boom" beat.

The crafts and activities bring everything together by reinforcing each theme. They can be worked into your storytime wherever you see fit, depending on your available time and the skill level of the children. I encourage you to use props and costumes whenever possible. Enlist parents who stay for storytime to help make the costumes. Puppets can also be made from old socks, inexpensive mittens, or garden gloves. Use the patterns in this book by enlarging or shrinking them to create flannel board or hand puppet pieces and adding Velcro to the backside.

Each storytime ends with the same song. This helps the children recognize when storytime is over. I also encourage you to post a newsletter (see sample on page 12) of what you have done during storytime, which will keep parents informed and motivate them to talk to their children about what they learned. You might also inform parents of upcoming themes, which might encourage them to dress their children a certain way or bring related items. Theme-appropriate snack ideas are also included.

Promoting Storytimes

The programs in this book are for schools, libraries, bookstores, recreation/park districts, scout troops, parents, grandparents, and anyone else who wants to promote the love of reading to children in a fun way. When planning a program, be sure to consider the age of the child and convenience for the parents. You might consider holding the program more than one time, offering an evening or weekend option or scheduling it when the children are out of school.

Getting the word out depends on your organization. Some ideas include:

- Posters to distribute to local businesses, such as Laundromats, grocery stores, local community agencies, and day care centers.

- Attach reminder slips to the posters, or have flyers to pass out so parents can post them at home.

- If you have a Web site, post all pertinent information on the site, listing the who, what, when, and where. Also post theme-related links to promote extended learning at home.

- Contact the local newspapers and ask them to post a community notice. Notifying your local newspaper of a community event might interest them enough to send a photographer and reporter. Or, you might ask what section would be appropriate for listing your event. Usually if you are a nonprofit organization, newspapers will include your information for free. Make sure you post your publicity in your scrapbook of events.

- Display a scrapbook that highlights all of the other special events you have done. This should contain pictures taken during your special day and any comments made by parents and participants. Any applicable promotional posters, newspaper articles, etc., can be included. Many scrapbooking businesses are now available; ask if they will assist you or do your scrapbook for you in exchange for free publicity (a sponsor thank-you).

- Exhibit any available props, your poster, and related materials available for checkout or sale. Set up your display where it will attract people's attention.

- Talk, talk, talk. Word of mouth is your best form of advertising.

- If you work at a library, go out into the community to day cares and other community agencies and present a quick "commercial" for your storytimes. Sing the song below and then leave current information on your storytimes.

I Love Books

Sung to the tune: "This Old Man"

I love books!
Yes-sir-ee!
They can make me ha-ap-py,
They can make me laugh,
They can help me go far.
I love books,
They're my shining star!

Oh, wow-whee!
The library,
I get lots of books for me,
I get songs and movies,
So much to see,
All for free,
At the library!

Planning a Storytime Program

Before Storytime

- Decide on your storytime theme and time frame. Then decide which books, activities, songs, and fingerplays you will use.

- Set the date and time and determine the number of children you would like to attend.

- Publicize your event.

- Search for props around your classroom, library, school, home, and community. You will be surprised by what people are willing to lend or give away. Resale shops are also a great resource.

- If you plan on serving a snack, let parents know so they can make you aware of any allergies.

- Obtain the books you will be reading.

- Copy the fingerplays and cut them out. Glue them to a 3½" x 5" index card so they are easier to see during storytime.

- Cut out and collect materials for art projects. Utilize older children, parents, grandparents, and volunteers from the community to assist.

- Prepare name tags. These are a great assistance not only to help you draw a child's attention to you or ask a question, but for the child to recognize letters, an important pre-reading skill.

Storytime

- Introduce the theme by asking the children about their name tags. Ask why they think these particular tags were chosen. "What could our stories be about?"

- Discuss the props and how they relate to the stories for the day. You may wish to play a version of "Who Am I?" before reading a story. For example, describe what animal might be in the next story you are about to read, then have the children guess what it could be. This is a good way to engage them before a story.

- Another way to let them know storytime is about to begin is to start with a familiar song. Here are two to choose from.

Sung to the tune: "I'm a Little Teapot"

We're all here for storytime,
What will we see?
Let's turn up our ears,
And they will be,
Ready to hear and listen well,
While we button our mouths as well.

Sung to the tune: "The Wheels on the Bus"

Our ears in Storytime,
Turn way up, *(Lightly twist earlobes with hands.)*
Turn way up,
Turn way up.
Our ears in storytime,
Turn way up,
So we can hear the stories.

Our mouths in storytime,
Wait to talk, *(Place fingers by lips, like "shhhhh.")*
Wait to talk,
Wait to talk.
Our mouths in storytime,
Wait to talk,
So we can hear the stories.

Our hands in storytime,
Fold on our laps, *(Exaggerate hand folding; bring hands to lap.)*
Fold on our laps,
Fold on our laps.
Our hands in storytime,
Fold on our laps,
Now let's read our stories! *(Open hands like a book.)*

- Read stories you have chosen and intersperse fingerplays and songs between the stories.

- Do any of the listed activities that fit within your theme and time frame.

- Lead a discussion with the children. Ask them what their favorite book was and what part they liked best. Depending on how many stories were read, you might have to help them remember. Ask them questions that are specific to the stories to reinforce comprehension concepts. A good time to talk to the children is when they are doing their art project.

- Become aware of the six skills for early literacy that the National Research Council and ALA promote. These skills are letter knowledge, print awareness, narrative skills, enriched vocabulary, print motivation, and phonological awareness. All of these skills are covered within the chapters of this book. An additional way to help with print awareness is to run your finger along the words as you read the title of a book. For more information, go to the ALA Web site at **www.ala.org** and type "six pre-reading skills" in the search box.

- Serve the storytime snack.

- Sing the goodbye song.

    Sung to the tune: "Twinkle, Twinkle, Little Star"

    We read great books today,
    Sang some songs along the way.
    Did some cool things, had some fun,

Sample Newsletter

Date

Dear Parents:

We had fun today with *(name theme)* in Storytime!

The stories we read today were:

(List titles and authors.)

There are many more great stories on this theme available for your children, and I encourage you to check out your local library or bookstore to share more with your child.

For art today we *(list project).*

We also *(list other activities you did, and explain how it helped their child, e.g., small motor skill development, pre-reading skills, basic math and science concepts, etc.).*

Here is a song/fingerplay we did today—ask your child to teach you! *(List a short one here.)*

I encourage you to discuss your child's Storytime experience with me. Please feel free to ask me any questions about possible ways to expand on what your child has done here today.

Thank you.

(Your name and center, library, etc.)

Back in Time
Medieval, Old West

Before Storytime

Name Tags

Copy the name tags on pages 27–28. Make enough copies so you have one name tag per child; cut out and list each child's name. You may wish to pin each name tag on with a safety pin, copy the name tags onto removable adhesive paper, or punch a hole in the top of each name tag and string it with yarn for a necklace.

Props

Medieval

Wear a plaid shirt and a different patterned pair of pants and a jester hat. Place bells on a string of yarn and shake. Make the Ye Old Parchment scroll on page 17. Carry it to announce the beginning of your storytime.

Of course, if you wish to be from more royal blood, you may wear a flowing dress (look for old prom dresses at resale shops) and a tiara or maiden's hat, made from a cardboard cone with an old scarf or shimmery material attached. Or, if you are to be a king, wear a bright red cloth or old blanket attached at the neck with old costume jewelry (again found at resale shops or rummage sales) and a crown (available for free at Burger King restaurants).

Old West

Jeans, a cowboy hat, and a simple shirt with a bandana could make you anything from a cowboy to a bandit. Stick horses are still available at toy stores and not only add a nice touch but can be used throughout your day's theme. Add a tin star (*make your own with cardboard and aluminum foil, get one at a toy or discount store, or ask a sheriff or police department for the ones they pass out to children*), and you could be the long arm of the law.

Storytime

- Introduce the theme by asking the children about their name tags.

- Show props and ask questions such as, "Who do you think wears clothes like this?" "Where would I have lived if I wore these types of clothes?" "What do you think our stories will be about today?"

- Sing the storytime song on page 10.

- Intersperse stories, songs, fingerplays, and activities that fit within your time frame.

Snack

Medieval
Snack foods of the time were pretzels, bagels, gingerbread, or gingersnaps. They also ate curds and whey (cottage cheese), porridge (oatmeal), grilled French bread (like French toast) with jam, and pocket pies (use refrigerator biscuits and fill with pie filing). Serve grape juice for wine or mead.

Old West
Travel foods of the time were limited to beef jerky, tack (hard, dry biscuits), and what they could find on the range (berries or animals). Instead serve biscuits with honey or gingersnaps (another food popular in the Old West), berries (blueberries, raspberries, blackberries, or mulberries), and hot cocoa for coffee.

Discussion Questions

Ask specific questions to reinforce comprehension concepts, re-ignite excitement for the stories shared, enrich children's vocabulary, and influence narrative skills.

For example:

- "What are some of the things Rapunzel throws down in *Falling for Rapunzel*?"

- "Do you remember what the 'Library Dragon' read that turns her into the librarian, in the book *The Library Dragon*?"

- "Who was the 'horse' in *A Wild Cowboy*?"

- "In *Cowboy Small* he branded the cattle. They do that to let everyone know it is their cattle. Can you think of another way they could mark them?"

- "Cowboy Roy did not ride a horse. What did he ride? Did they have bicycles in the Old West?"

Songs

Medieval

If I Were a Princess

Sung to the tune: "All Around the Mulberry Bush"

I'd love to be a princess,
And live in a castle,
Have maids, and jesters, and a crown, too.
Wow, there's a knight!

He helps to guard our kingdom,
From all who would harm it,
Lots of people to keep safe,
So he wears his armor.

My father is a king and
My mother is a queen,
I'll marry a prince someday,
And live happily ever after!

Royal Family

Sung to the tune: "Make New Friends" (Girl Scout Traditional)

I am a king,
I wear a crown.
My wife is queen,
All the peasants bow down.

My son is a prince,

My daughter, princess.
We are all royalty,
You know by how we dress.

I Am a King

Sung to the tune: "Skip to My Lou"

I have a throne,
I'm a king you see.
I have a scepter, yes sirree,
I have a wife, she's queen Bea,
We live very royally.

Old West

Oh, I Wish I Were a Rowdy Cowgirl

Author Unknown

Sung to the tune: Oscar Mayer Song

Oh, I wish I were a rowdy cowgirl,
That is what I'd truly like to be.
'Cause if I were a rowdy cowgirl,
No old steer would get away from me!

Oh, I wish I were a tough old cowgirl,
That is what I'd truly like to be.
'Cause if I were a tough old cowgirl,
All the men would be afraid of me!

Oh, I wish I were a sharpshooting cowgirl,
That is what I'd truly like to be.
'Cause if I were a sharpshooting cowgirl
Then I could be like Annie Oakley!

Home on the Range

Traditional

Oh give me a home, where the buffalo roam,
And the deer and the antelope play.
Where seldom is heard, a discouraging word,
And the sky is not cloudy all day.
Home, home on the range,
Where the deer and the antelope play,
Where seldom is heard, a discouraging word,
And the skies are not cloudy all day.

At the Rodeo

Author Unknown

Sung to the tune: "Mary Had a Little Lamb"

I will ride around the ring, *(Trot in a circle.)*
Around the ring, around the ring.
I will ride around the ring,
At the rodeo today.

Next I'll ride a bucking bronco,
(Leap and prance.)
A bucking bronco, a bucking bronco,
Next I'll ride a bucking bronco,
Around the rodeo ring.

Last I'll try to rope a steer,
(Pretend to throw a rope.)
Rope a steer, rope a steer.
Next I'll try to rope a steer,
At the rodeo today!

Little Cowpoke

Author Unknown

Sung to the tune: "I'm a Little Teapot"

I'm a little cowpoke,
(Point to self.)
With a horse so tall.
(Hold arms above head and look up.)
But my hat's too big,
(Pull pretend hat down over ears.)
And my boots too small.
(Walk as if feet hurt.)

I want to rope some cattle,
(Pretend to throw a lasso.)
But I'm afraid I'll fall.
(Show a worried face.)
So I'll just wait'll next year,
(Wave goodbye.)
To ride with y'all!
(Pretend to hold horse's reins.)

Be a Cowboy

Sung to the tune: "Do Your Ears Hang Low?"

Would you like to ride,
On a horse, under the sky?
Could you help us go,
Get the cattle from the snow?
Will you ride all day,
Till the steer are safe away?
Would you be a cowboy?

Fingerplays

Medieval

Here Is the Prince

Here is the knight so strong and true,
(Hold up index finger.)

Here is the king, he rules for you. *(Hold up middle finger next to index finger and bend finger.)*

Here is the queen, bow as she goes past. *(Hold up ring finger next to above fingers and bend to bow.)*

Here is the prince, he will one day rule,
(Hold up pinky finger next to others.)

Among the land so green and vast.
(Spread hands out, palms up.)

Old West

I'm a Buckaroo

I'm a buckaroo, *(Point to self.)*
I'm as happy as can be. *(Smile.)*
I ride upon my horse, *(Pretend to ride a horse.)*
So all the west I'll see.
(Place hand over eyes, look around.)

I drive the cattle from here to there,
(Point here and there.)
Giving them water and food,
While I remain aware, *(Look around excitedly.)*
Of all the dangers there might be,
Like coyotes, or bandits I may need to flee.
(Place hand over mouth and nose, squint, fling hand away.)

As I ride to the ranch,
I must sleep under the stars,
(Place hands on the side of your head, tilt head.)
'Cause in my day there are no cars.
(Shake head.)
Just my horse and me, riding long and far,
(Pretend to ride a horse.)
Following that distant star, *(Point to the stars.)*
Back towards the old homestead,
Where I can sleep in my own bed. *(Place hands on the side of your head, tilt head.)*

Craft Activities

Medieval

Milk Cap Brooches

Supplies needed:

- milk caps
- safety pin 1½" in length *
- lace
- glue
- beads and jewels **
- wallpaper

Directions:

1. Glue the lace on or around the top of the milk cap.
2. Glue the wallpaper to the lace.
3. Glue on beads and jewels.
4. Place the safety pin in the back of milk cap, wedged under the ridges.
5. Wear like royalty!

   * To keep this a safe project, give the parents the safety pin separate from their child's brooch. Show them how easily it pops in and out of the back of the milk cap.

   ** Use old inexpensive necklaces and cut them apart for beads.

Jester Sticks

Supplies needed:

- 3 pieces of ribbon per person ⅛" wide by 6–8" long (vary in length)
- 1 thick Popsicle stick per person
- jewel beads/sequins
- colored pencils or markers
- felt
- scissors
- beads
- jester pattern on page 26 (two per child)
- glue

Directions:

1. Color the jester heads.
2. Cut out felt for the jester's mantel.

3. Add beads to the ends of the ribbons.
4. Glue the end of the ribbons, felt, and jester heads to the top of the Popsicle stick.
5. Color or decorate both sides of the Popsicle stick with markers, colored pencils or sequins, and jewel beads.
6. Twist and twirl your jester stick as you tell a joke; laugh as you hop on one foot; entertain in any way that will make people smile!

Stained Glass Window Panes

Supplies needed:

- various colors of tissue paper
- cardboard
- scissors
- glue

Directions:

1. Cut one end of a piece of cardboard in an arch shape. You determine the size by how long you would like the project to take. A nice size is 4½" x 6½".
2. Fold the cardboard in half and cut various shapes into the "window" arch. To help the colors really show through, cut a larger shape in the center. Assist the children so they do not cut too close to the edge; the frame needs to remain uncut. *
3. Once the desired design has been cut into the cardboard, glue pieces of tissue paper over the cut-out areas.
4. The result is a beautiful array of colors that creates a nice sun catcher.

   * Give the children a guide by coloring a ⅛" black border around the edge of the cardboard with a black marker. This also aids in the look of a "window."

Medieval Tunics

Supplies needed:

- 1 paper grocery bag per person
- scissors
- crayons/markers
- tape (just in case)

Directions:

1. Cut an oval-shaped hole in the bottom of a paper grocery bag.

2. Cut out a triangle on each side of the bag, leaving only 3 inches on the bottom.

3. Cut out rectangles at the top of the bag.

4. If you have imprinting on the outside of the bag, carefully turn the bag inside out.

5. In what is now the open end and front of your tunic, cut out three rectangles, which will form a type of mantle design.

6. Decorate the front and back with markers or crayons.

7. Have crest designs, coat of arms, and pictures of medieval tunics so the children can see what designs were on tunics in medieval times.

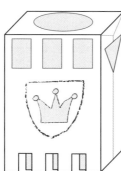

Dragon Puppet

Supplies needed:

- paper towel tube
- green tissue paper
- tape
- small piece of red felt
- green construction paper (two full sheets for each project)
- black marker
- scissors
- glue

Directions:

1. From one end of the paper towel tube, cut a long oval approximately 2" long. Cut a fang at each end of the oval.

2. About ½ inch behind the first cut, cut an oval-shaped hole large enough for your finger to go through.

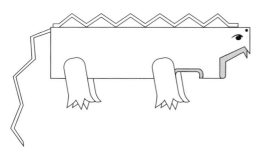

3. Cover the paper towel tube with green tissue, leaving the holes exposed.

4. Fold one piece of green construction paper lengthwise in an accordion fashion. Tape the accordion to the top of the tube to form the dragon scales.

5. Fold another piece of construction paper horizontally in an accordion fashion, so it is about 1" wide. Cut the end in a "V" shape, then tape it inside the back of the tube. This is the tail.

6. Cut four legs from the tissue and glue them to the sides of the dragon's body.

7. Use the black marker to draw on two eyes and nostrils.

8. Cut the small piece of red felt into a triangle. Cut slits across the top of the pointed edge.

9. Fold the wide end of the triangle over your finger and tape, glue, or sew it together. This is the dragon's fire.

10. Place the felt around your finger and pop it in and out of the mouth as the dragon breaths fire.

Ye Old Parchment Scroll

Supplies needed:

- 2 paper towel tubes per project
- tape
- ledger size paper
- tea bags (the kind without tags work best)
- markers
- scissors
- aluminum foil
- paint (*optional*)
- jewel beads/sequins

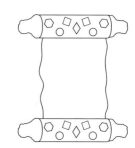

Directions:

1. Crumple the paper, then flatten it.

2. Cut the sides of the paper in a "wavy" fashion.

3. Soak the tea bags in a small amount of warm water.

4. Cut a slit in the paper towel tube just long enough to fit the edge of the paper through the tube.

5. Place a small piece of tape on the edge of the paper and slide through the slit. Rub the edge to affix the tape to the inside of the tube.

6. Squeeze the tea bags so they are damp but not wet and have the children pat them onto the paper.

7. Use aluminum foil to create the scroll knobs.

8. Cover the paper towel tube (scroll rod) with aluminum foil and tuck the edges into the slit, affixing with tape on the inside of the tube.

9. Glue on jewel beads and/or sequins.

10. Have the children write their message on the parchment paper.

Options:
To make a plainer scroll, paint the paper towel tube or decorate it with markers.

To write an invisible message, use lemon juice. Place the message under a warm light to read it.

Old West

Watercolor

Supplies needed:

- stamper
- watercolors and brushes
- paper

Directions:

In the Old West, artists painted with watercolors to portray scenes of cowboys, landscapes, and wildlife.

1. Use the picture on page 25. Copy one for each child.

2. After reading *Cowboy Small,* have each child "brand" the horse with a small stamper.

3. Have the children paint their pictures.

Pony Express Mail Pouches

Supplies needed:

- small brown paper lunch bags (2 per project, plus extras)
- glue
- buttons (4 per project)
- markers/crayons
- small rubber bands (2 per project)
- stickers *(optional)*

Directions:

1. Open the two bags and fold down the tops approximately 3 inches.

2. On the back of each bag, about one inch down from the fold, cut two vertical slits about 2 inches long and 2 inches apart.

3. Using another bag, cut a strip about 1¼ inches wide down the length of the bag. (This is the saddlebag strap.) Slip one end through the slot and out the other side. Repeat with the other bag. Tape the ends together.

4. Glue a button toward the edge of the folded flap and underneath the fold on the front of both bags.

5. While the glue dries, decorate the bags using crayons, markers, and stickers if desired.

6. Fill the pouches with mail, then wrap a small rubber band around the buttons in a figure eight fashion.

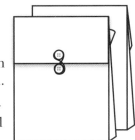

7. Ride off into the sunset to deliver the mail across the range!

Branded Bandannas

Supplies needed:

- square piece of cloth or men's white handkerchief (one per project)
- fabric paint
- potatoes (1 or more)
- knife
- Styrofoam meat or vegetable trays

Directions:

1. Cut the potato in half and carve out a shape, such as a star, "s," or lightning bolt.

2. Put paint in Styrofoam trays.

3. Give each child a piece of cloth; have them stamp (brand) their bandanna by dipping the potato in the paint and pressing it onto the fabric.

Gross Motor Activities

Medieval

Jester Training

Supplies needed:

- juggling balls
- jester hat (*optional*)
- wrist or ankle bells

Directions:

1. Have the children sit in a circle.

2. One child puts on the bells and hat and stands in the middle of the circle.

3. The child in the middle tries to juggle while the other children in the circle suggest additional activities to do at the same time, such as jumping, standing on one foot, turning, waving one hand up high, prancing, etc.

Old West

Bucking Bronco Roping Arena

Supplies needed:

- oatmeal containers (or chairs)
- broom or stick horse
- light rope (clothesline weight works well), approximately 4 feet long
- stuffed animals (preferably cows or horses, but imagination is key here)

Directions:

1. Set up the oatmeal containers (barrels) or chairs in a fashion resembling an obstacle course.

2. Place the stuffed animals on the floor around, but off to the side of, the barrels.

3. Tie a knot in the rope so there is a loop at one end large enough to fit around the stuffed animals.

4. Have each child "ride" the bronco (broom) around the barrels and "lasso" the cattle (stuffed animals). Make sure the other children stand at a safe distance for the child to toss the rope. The object is to see how close they can get to ringing the animal (tossing the rope around it)—the rope does not have to tighten around the animal.

Horseshoes

Supplies needed:

- aluminum foil
- cardboard
- paper towel tube
- Styrofoam meat tray

Directions:

1. Cut the cardboard in horseshoe shapes. *

2. Cover the horseshoes with aluminum foil.

3. Cut a hole slightly smaller than the size of the paper towel tube in the middle of the meat tray and place the tube in the center.

4. Have the children stand back (whatever distance you choose) and toss the horseshoes towards the "stake" trying for a "ringer."

   * You can also use the horseshoes fashioned by the children on page 21.

Cowboy/Cowgirl Relay

Supplies needed:

- cowboy hats
- vests
- bandannas
- cowboy boots in various sizes
- work gloves
- two large bags
- cowboy shirts

Directions:

1. Have all of the children line up in two lines.

2. Place one bag with a variety of clothes in it at the other end of the room.

3. Have the children, one at a time, walk quickly to the bag and put on all the clothes in the bag.

4. When they are fully dressed, have them shout "yippee-yah-yeah!"

5. Continue until every child has had a turn.

6. The children who are waiting in line can "clip-clop" out a beat as if riding a horse, either by patting their thighs, making the sound with their mouths, or using their feet.

Math & Science Activities

Medieval

Homemade Butter

Supplies needed:

- whipping cream
- salt
- container with a screw tight lid
- lots of hands and muscles

Directions:

1. Pour some whipping cream in the container, add a small amount of salt, and screw tight the lid. (The amount of cream is not important, just allow for room to shake the cream.)

2. Pass the container around and have the children shake the container.

3. As the children are shaking the cream, explain how in medieval times grocery stores did not exist. People did not have a place to buy food; instead, they made food on their farms and survived off of the land and what the animals could give them.

4. Ask questions such as: "What animal gives us cream?" "What color is the cream now?" "What color will the cream be when it turns to butter?"

5. Explain that the butter will become yellow because the fat in the cream all comes together, and fat is naturally yellow. Show the children a picture of a butter churn, explaining that people back

then used it to make butter because it allowed them to make larger amounts at once. Explain also that temperature was a factor in how well the cream would turn into butter. If it was too hot, it would be too soft and fluffy. If it was too cold, it lumped into balls and would not stick together.

Old West

Lassoing

Supplies needed:

- rope

Directions:

1. Show a lasso rope and have the children measure its length with different things from around the room, as well as their bodies.

2. Ask questions such as, "Is it longer than your leg?" "Your whole body?"

3. Discuss how horses are measured in hands. How many hands high are they? Discuss what the average height of a horse is and compare to how tall you and the children are.

Fine Motor Skills Activities

Medieval

Embroidery

Supplies needed:

- cardboard with either a design drawn or glued on it, or ready-made sewing cards
- hole punch
- shoelaces
- a piece of embroidery for discussion

Directions:

1. Show the children some completed embroidered pieces. Explain that this was a craft done during medieval times by women and girls.

2. If you are making your own sewing cards, draw or glue a picture on the cardboard. Use a hole punch around the edges for the shoelace to be put through. Tie the shoelace through one end of the hole, where you want the children to begin.

3. Show the children how to go in and out with the end of the shoestring to follow a pattern.

Combing Wool

Supplies needed:

- 2 metal-toothed dog brushes
- raw wool (*Available online very inexpensively. Type in "raw wool" on any search engine. Another option is to ask a local sheep farmer for a small amount.*)

Directions:

1. Place a piece of raw wool between two metal brushes.

2. Drag the brushes in opposite directions and continue combing until the wool becomes soft and fluffy. Show the children that they may pull left and right, or up and down.

3. Try it as a team with one child holding one brush and another child dragging it across the top. Ask the children to think of different ways they could try to comb the wool.

4. Discuss the concepts with the children as they take turns. Use vocabulary words like soft, matted, fluffy, drag, pull, left, right, up, down, etc. Explain any words that might be unfamiliar to the children. This is not only a fine motor activity, but also an opportunity for pre-literacy skill development.

Old West

Panning for Gold

Supplies needed:

- dishpan
- rocks
- gold nuggets (available at a novelty store, or create your own by spray painting small rocks gold)
- small aluminum pans

Directions:

1. Place a small amount of water in the dishpan.

2. Add rocks and gold nuggets.

3. Allow the children to "pan" for gold using the small aluminum pans.

Horseshoeing

Supplies needed:

- aluminum foil
- small wooden mallet or hammer (a meat mallet works well, too)

Directions:

1. Give each child a piece of aluminum foil.

2. Have them roll, shape, and pound it into a horseshoe shape.

Storytime Books to Share

Books about Medieval Times

Alice the Fairy by David Shannon. Blue Sky Press, 2004. Alice has a nose for trouble, but luckily she's a fairy—a Temporary Fairy. She has a magic wand, fairy wings, and a blanket, all of which she uses to disappear, to fly, to transform her dad into a horse, and to turn his cookies into her own! There are still a few things Alice needs to learn to become a Permanent Fairy, like how to float her dog on the ceiling and make her clothes put themselves away, but she's working on it—sort of.

Arthur's Tractor: A Fairy Tale with Mechanical Parts by Pippa Goodhart. Bloomsbury, 2003. Unaware that a princess in distress and a dragon on the loose are right behind him, Arthur the farmer thinks that the strange noises he keeps hearing are being made by his tractor breaking down.

The Best Pet of All by David LaRochelle. Dutton, 2004. A little boy asks his mother for a pet dog, but she says no. After she agrees to a pet dragon, she decides to rethink her choice of a pet.

Do Knights Take Naps? by Kathy Tucker. Albert Whitman, 2000. Rhyming text explores what it means to be a knight, what he wears, and what he does for fun.

Do Princesses Wear Hiking Boots? by Carmela LaVigna Coyle. Rising Moon, 2003. When a little girl asks her mother about princesses, she learns that they are much like herself.

The Egg by M. P. Robertson. Dial, 2001. George hatches a dragon from a strange egg that he finds and then faces the challenge of raising him properly.

Falling For Rapunzel by Leah Wilcox. Putnam, 2003. The prince is hoping to fall for Rapunzel, but since she can't quite hear what he asks for, everything but her hair gets tossed out her window. Instead of her curly locks, she throws her dirty socks. Instead of silky tresses, out go lacy dresses. Finally Rapunzel heaves out something that makes all the prince's dreams come true, showing how misunderstandings can lead to happily-ever-after.

The Great Dragon Rescue by M. P. Robertson. Dial, 2004. In this companion to the popular picture book *The Egg*, George and his dragon are reunited. One morning George is moping around the chicken coop, daydreaming of adventure, when suddenly his dragon friend swoops out of the sky and carries him off ... to a deep, dark forest. There they spy on a wicked witch who has captured a baby dragon! Papa dragon needs George's help, and it's up to him to think of a clever rescue—and fast. Luckily, when it comes to fighting bad magic, George has a few tricks up his sleeve.

I Am Really a Princess by Carol Diggory Shields. Puffin, 1996. A child imagines herself a princess and contrasts her everyday life with the one she could have in a castle with infinitely permissive parents.

Knight and the Dragon by Tomie de Paola. Putnam, 1998. A knight who has never fought a dragon and an equally inexperienced dragon prepare to meet each other in battle.

The Library Dragon by Carmen A. Deedy. Peachtree Publishers, 1994. Miss Lotta Scales is a dragon who believes her job is to protect the school's library books from the children, but when she finally realizes that books are meant to be read, the dragon turns into Miss Lotty, librarian and storyteller.

Lullabyhullaballoo! by Mick Inkpen. Hodder Children's Books, 1993. A princess has trouble getting to sleep, until some clanking knights, snorting dragons, eerie ghosts, and forest creatures come to her aid.

The Missing Tarts by B. G. Hennessy. Viking, 1989. When the Queen of Hearts discovers that her strawberry tarts have been stolen, she enlists the help of many popular nursery rhyme characters in order to find them.

Paper Bag Princess by Robert Munsch. Annick Press, 1980. Elizabeth, a beautiful princess, lives in a castle and wears fancy clothes. Just when she is about to marry Prince Ronald, a dragon smashes her castle, burns her clothes with his fiery breath, and prince-naps her dear Ronald. Undaunted and presumably unclad, she dons a large paper bag and sets off to find the dragon and her cherished prince. Once she's tracked down the rascally reptile, she flatters him into performing all sorts of dragonfly stunts that eventually exhaust him, allowing her to rescue Prince Ronald. But what does Prince Not-So-Charming say when he sees her? In any case, let's just say that Princess Elizabeth and Prince Ronald do not, under any circumstances, live happily ever after.

The Princess Knight by Cornelia Funke. Scholastic, 2001. Violetta is a little princess who wishes she could be big and strong like her brothers. But what she lacks in size she makes up for in determination.

Raising Dragons by Jerdine Nolen. Silver Whistle, 1998. A farmer's young daughter shares numerous adventures with the dragon that she raises from infancy.

There's a Dragon in My Sleeping Bag by James Howe. Aladdin, 1998. Alex is intimidated by his older brother Simon's imaginary dragon, until he is able to create his own friend—a camel named Calvin.

There's No Such Thing As a Dragon by Jack Kent. Golden Books, 2005. Billy Bixbee awakens to find a dragon "about the size of a kitten" sitting on his bed. The dragon grows by leaps and bounds, until Billy dares to pet the attention-seeking creature and it shrinks back down into an adoring little lap dragon.

Books about the Old West

Armadillo Rodeo by Jan Brett. Putnam, 1995. When Bo spots what he thinks is a "rip-roarin', rootin'-tootin', shiny red armadillo," he knows what he has to do. Follow that armadillo! Bo leaves his mother and three brothers behind and takes off for a two-stepping, bronco-bucking adventure.

Birthday Mice! by Bethany Roberts. Clarion Books, 2002. When a mouse turns two, his friends and family throw a cowboy theme party.

B is for Buckaroo: A Cowboy Alphabet by Louise Doak Whitney and Gleaves Whitney. Sleeping Bear Press, 2003. The letters of the alphabet are represented by words and set in short rhymes with additional information relating to cowboys and ranch life.

Cinderdog and the Wicked Stepcat by Joan Holub. Albert Whitman, 2001. When Cowboy Carl marries Cactus Kate, Carl's dog, Cinderdog, must deal with his new sibling, Kate's ornery cat, Wicked.

Cowboy and His Friend by Joan Walsh Anglund. Harcourt Brace, 1961. Reprinted in 2002. A cowboy's bear is a very special friend who is always with him, no matter where he goes or what he does.

Cowboy Dreams by Kathi Appelt. HarperCollins, 1999. A little cowpoke is lulled to sleep by dreams of the sights and sounds of the Western landscape at night.

Cowboy Kid by Max Eilenberg. Candlewick Press, 2000. A young boy has difficulty getting to sleep because his toys seem to need so many hugs and kisses at bedtime.

Cowboy Pup by Carole Etow. Golden Press, 1993. Describes the day in the life of Cowboy Pup, with an eye-catching furry face attached.

Cowboy Roy by Cathy East Dubowski and Mark Dubowski. Grossett & Dunlap, 2000. Roy, a young cowboy, tries hard to ride his bicycle without the training wheels.

Cowboys by Glen Rounds. Holiday House, 1991. Follows a cowboy from sunup to bedtime as he rounds up cattle, kills a rattlesnake, and plays cards in the bunkhouse after dinner.

Cowboy Small by Lois Lenski. Random House, 2001. Cowboy Small does it all. Whether it's rounding up cattle for branding, taking care of his horse, or singing songs by the chuck wagon, he knows how to be a cowboy.

Cowboy Up! by Larry Dane Brimner. Scholastic Library Publishing, 1999. Presents a rhyming look at a cowboy's day at the rodeo.

Cowgirl Rosie and Her Five Baby Bison by Stephen Gulbis. Little, Brown and Company, 2001. Cowgirl Rosie takes her five baby bison everywhere. But one day, on the way to visit the sheriff, every one of them—Bigwig, Bonnie, Beefy, Butch, and even little Baby B—disappears! Will Cowgirl Rosie and Sheriff Joe be able to outsmart sneaky Snakey Jake and get her baby bison back?

Dusty Locks and the Three Bears by Susan Lowell and Randy Cecil. Henry Holt & Company. 2001. A western-style retelling of the traditional tale about a little girl who finds the house of a bear family and makes herself at home.

I Want to Be a Cowboy by Dan Liebman. Firefly Books, 1999. Real pictures depict everyday life as a cowboy.

Joe Cinders by Marianne Mitchell. Henry Holt & Company, 2002. With a "hot diggety dog!" and a wave of his white sombrero, cowboy Joe Cinders gets the girl in this Southwestern retelling of the Cinderella story.

Lasso Lou and Cowboy McCoy by Barbara Larmon Failing. Dial, 2003. McCoy buys himself a cowboy hat, which leads to a new career and a series of misadventures at the Bo-Dee-Oh-Ranch.

Matthew the Cowboy by Ruth Hooker. Albert Whitman, 1990. After receiving a cowboy suit for his birthday, Matthew takes an imaginary trip out West where he tames a wild horse, solves a puzzle of a mysterious cattle brand, and captures some rustlers.

Mustang Canyon by Jonathan London. Candlewick Press, 2002. A young mustang is separated from its mother when a plane swoops over the canyon.

The Old Chisholm Trail by Rosalyn Schanzer. National Geographic Society, 2001. An illustrated version of the legendary song. The many verses were made up by cowboys while herding cattle on the Chisholm Trail.

The One that Got Away by Percival Everett. Clarion Books, 1992. Three cowhands chase and corral horses in this zany book about the Wild West.

Pug, Slug, and Doug the Thug by Carol Saller. Carolrhoda Books, 1994. A humorous Wild West tale, told in verse, about a dog, a cat, and a lone boy who team up to outwit the villainous bad guys Pug, Slug, and Doug the Thug.

She'll Be Comin' 'Round the Mountain by Philemon Sturges. Little, Brown and Company, 2004. New words to the traditional tune describe a camper-driven "hootin" and "shoutin" guest and the party that will begin when she arrives.

Sixteen Cows by Lisa Wheeler. Harcourt, 2002. Rhyming tale of Cowboy Gene and Cowgirl Sue, whose beloved cows get mixed up when a storm blows down the fence between their ranches.

A Wild Cowboy by Dana Kessimakis. Hyperion, 2004. When a little boy gets set to spend the day at Grandma's, he's really preparing to go on the cowboy ride of his dreams. With his imagination in tow, he and his partner (brother) ride their horses (Mom and Dad) to meet their ranch hand (Grandma). After having a great day doing all the things that cowfolk do, this fantastic adventure ends in a wonderfully reassuring way as the cowboy and his "horse" are reunited, just in time to be tucked in bed.

Additional Resources

Old West

National Cowgirl Museum and Hall of Fame
1720 Gendy St.
Fort Worth, TX 76107
1-800-476-FAME (3263)

- Free for educators: Traveling Trunks & Saddlebags. Includes artifacts, photos, books for all ages, rope tricks, bibliographies, teacher's manual, and related activities. Go to **www.cowgirl.net,** click on the "Education" link and go to the "Traveling Trunk & Saddlebags" link.

Pattern for Watercolor Activity

Pattern for Jester Sticks

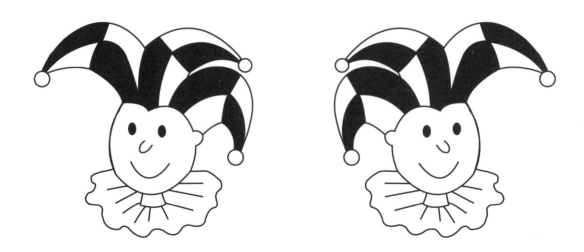

Name Tag Patterns for Back In Time

Name Tag Patterns for Back In Time

Beach Days
Oceans & Ocean Life, Sand & Sun

Before Storytime

Name Tags

Copy the name tags on pages 38–40. Make enough copies so you have one name tag per child; cut out and list each child's name. You may wish to pin each name tag on with a safety pin, copy the name tags onto removable adhesive paper, or punch a hole in the top of each name tag and string it with yarn for a necklace.

Props

- Wear summer clothes, a floppy beach or sun hat, flip-flops, and sunglasses (the really large clown kind are a great attention getter).

- Carry a basket with sunscreen, a frisbee, sand shovel or bucket, a water bottle, and your books in it.

- Drape a towel over your shoulders and you are ready for the beach!

Storytime

- Introduce the theme by asking the children about their name tags.

- Show props and ask questions such as, "Where do I look like I'm headed?" "What do you like to do at the beach?"

- Sing the storytime song on page 10.

- Intersperse stories, songs, fingerplays, and activities that fit within your time frame.

Snack

Beach Salads and Smoothies

Supplies needed:

- clean hands!

- clean vegetable or meat trays (yellow or blue for sand or water)—1 per child

- fruits: apples, bananas, pineapple, berries, etc.

- plastic knives

- pretzel sticks

- celery stalks with the leaves on

- mushroom caps

- croutons

- peanut butter

- cherry tomatoes

- ranch dressing

Directions:

1. For smoothies:
   Have a variety of fresh fruit available. Allow the children to help cut up some of the softer fruits and place them in the blender.

2. For beach salads:
   Place a small dab of peanut butter in two places on the tray and have the children place the celery stalk on one for a palm tree and a pretzel stick with a mushroom cap on top for a beach umbrella.

   Pour a small amount of ranch dressing on the tray for the sand area.

   Place cherry tomatoes on the tray for beach balls.

   Give them croutons to build a sand castle. Enjoy the tasty beach scene—yum!

Discussion Questions

Ask specific questions to reinforce comprehension concepts, re-ignite excitement for the stories shared, enrich children's vocabulary, and influence narrative skills.

For example:

- "Name some of the things that happen to Roxanne in *How Will We Get to the Beach?* What are some of the things she wanted to bring to the beach? How does she finally get to the beach?"

- "Tell me some of the adventures they have on the way to the beach in *Beach Day?*"

- "The man at the pet store told the boy not to do something in *A Fish Out of Water;* what was it?"

- "What animal wants to swim in the book *Sink or Swim?*"

- "In *Bear's Adventure,* what are some of the things that happened to him, and does he get back home?"

Wrapping It Up

Sing the song on page 11.

Songs

At the Beach

Sung to the tune: "When the Saints Go Marching"

We're on the beach.
We're on the beach.
We're on the beach, and the sand's very hot!
How would your feet react?
To the sand, on the hot beach. *(Jump up and down, one foot at a time.)*

We're in the water.
We're in the water.
We're in the cold, wet, water.
How would you react in the water?
When it feels icy cold. *(Shiver, wrap arms around self.)*

We're in the sun.
We're in the sun.
We're in the warm sun, on the beach.
How would you feel on the beach?
In the warm, bright sunshine. *(See how children react, smile!)*

Waves at the Beach

Author Unknown

Sung to the tune: "The Wheels on the Bus"

The waves at the beach go up and down,
Up and down, up and down,
The waves at the beach go up and down,
All day long. *(Stand and raise arms overhead and then sit.)*

The lobsters on the beach go snap, snap, snap,
Snap, snap, snap, snap, snap, snap,
The lobsters on the beach go snap, snap, snap,
All day long. *(Snap fingers or clap hands.)*

The crabs on the beach go back and forth,
Back and forth, back and forth,
The crabs on the beach go back and forth,
All day long. *(Wiggle your fingers as you bring your hand across your left to right.)*

The clams on the beach will open and shut,
Open and shut, open and shut,
The clams on the beach will open and shut,
All day long. *(Open and shut hands.)*

The jellyfish they go wibble, wobble, wibble,
Wibble, wobble, wibble,
Wibble, wobble, wibble,
The jellyfish they go wibble, wobble, wibble,
All day long. *(Wiggle hands and flip hand over.)*

The Octopus

Author Unknown

Sung to the tune: "Little White Duck"

There are eight tentacles,
Swimming in the ocean,
Eight tentacles making a commotion.
Who could belong to so many feet?

The octopus does and they help him eat.
He has eight tentacles,
Swimming in the ocean.
Swim, swim, swim.

Let's Go to the Beach

Author Unknown

Sung to the tune: "A Hunting We Will Go"

Let's go to the beach,
To swim and play and run.
Building castles in the sand,
Is ever so much fun.

Be sure to wear your suit,
And bring along your float.
We'll ride so far out in the surf,
Pretending it's a boat.

We'll find some pretty shells,
And throw the gulls some bread.
Put on a lot of suntan lotion,
So we don't turn red.

We'll never want to leave,
Such fun this has been.
But we'll come another day,
And do it all again!

Seagull Song

Author Unknown

Sung to the tune: "Frére Jacques"

I see seagulls,
I see seagulls,
At the beach.
At the beach.

Soaring, fishing, diving,
Soaring, fishing, diving,
At the beach.
At the beach.

I hear the ocean,
I hear the ocean,
At the beach.
At the beach.

Crashing, splashing, foaming,
Crashing, splashing, foaming,
At the beach.
At the beach.

Take Me Out to the Ocean

Author Unknown

Sung to the tune: "Take Me Out to the Ballgame"

Take me out to the ocean,
Take me out to the sea.
There goes a starfish and sand dollar,
I'm having such fun; I've just got to holler!

Oh, it's swim, swim, swim, underwater,
Catch a ride on a whale.
For the sand is a great place to be,
With my shovel and pail.

To the Beach

Author Unknown

Sung to the tune: "London Bridges"

We are going to the beach,
To the beach, to the beach.
We are going to the beach,
In our swimsuits.

We will find rocks and shells,
Rocks and shells, rocks and shells.
We will find rocks and shells,
Gathered by the water.

We will build a sand castle ...
With bridges and a tower.

We will have a picnic too ...
With sandwiches and oranges.

Home we head with sunburned cheeks ...
And treasures from the ocean.

I Love the Beach

Sung to the tune: "California Girls" (Beach Boys song)

Well I love the beach,
The warm sunshine,
The wind in my hair.
And the seagulls flying all around,
Way up in the air.

Chorus:
I wish I could be at the beach always.

Echo:
I wish I could be at the beach always,
Be like a fish,
And swim beneath the waves.

Splish, Splash! I'm Going to the Beach

Sung to the tune: "Splish Splash"

Wow! Whee! I'm going to the sea,
I get to swim and play!
Having fun in the sand and the sun,
Thinking I could last all day!

I'm a swimmin' with the fishes,
And playing in the sea,
Thinking I'm as happy as I ever can be!

Then, splish, splash!
I was told I gotta go,
How was I to know,
I wouldn't get to see the show?

There would be sunsets and moonlight.
And stars out that are so bright!
But, oh well, I brought back a shell,
So now I can remember what a great day I had.

And come back to do some splashin',
And see the waves a crashin',
Then I'll come back,
To the beach someday,
With my swimming suit on—yeah!

Fingerplays

Once I Saw an Octopus

Author Unknown

Once I saw an octopus,
In the deep blue sea. *(Point downward.)*
I called, "Mr. Octopus, *(Cup hands by mouth.)*
Won't you swim with me?"
Then out came his tentacles,
So very long and straight, *(Extend eight fingers.)*
One, two, three, and four, *(Count on fingers.)*
Five and six and seven and eight.

Little Fishy

Author Unknown

See the little fishy, *(Place forefingers together.)*
Swimming in the sea? *(Wiggle hand.)*
Wiggle, wiggle goes his tail, *(Wiggle hand.)*
As he swims by me. *(Point to self.)*
My face is in the water, *(Cup hands around face
and bend down.)*
And what do you suppose? *(Shrug.)*
That squiggly little fish, *(Wiggle hand.)*
Nipped me in the nose! *(Pinch fingers on nose.)*

The Beach

Author Unknown

Bring your swimsuit and a pail, *(Beckon with
hand; pretend to hold a pail.)*

Maybe we will catch a whale! *(Place palms
together; wriggle wrists and spread arms out wide.)*

How can the beach sand be so hot?
(Jump and hop.)

When the waves in the water are not!
(Point to toes, and then shiver.)

Sand Castles

Author Unknown

I dug in the sand, *(Pretend to dig.)*
And I carefully made,
Five sand castles, *(Hold up five fingers.)*
With my pail and spade.

I felt like a king, *(queen)*
In a golden crown,
(Place hands in a circle above head.)
Till the blue sea, *(Make waves with hands.)*
Knocked my castles down. *(Move both hands
out; palms down.)*

So I dug again, *(Pretend to dig.)*
In that sandy shore,
Till I had ten castles more, *(Hold up ten fingers.)*
And I was a king, *(queen)*
(Place hands in a circle above head.)
Once more. *(Stand tall.)*

Five Little Fish

Author Unknown

Note: *Use name tags from pages 172 as flannel
board pieces with this fingerplay, or just hold up
appropriate number of fingers.*

Five little fish, swimming by the shore,
One got caught, and now there were four.
Four little fish, swimming in the sea,
One got caught, and now there were three.
Three little fish, swimming in the blue,
One got caught, and now there were two.
Two little fish, swimming in the sun,
One got caught, and now there was one.
One little fish, swimming for home,
Decided it was best never to roam.

I Walked to the Beach

Author Unknown

I walked to the beach,
(Swing arms and walk in place.)
And what did I see? *(Put hands over eyes, looking.)*
A lot of little fishes, *(Place hands together; wig-
gle.)*
Looking at me! *(Point to self.)*

I jumped into the water, *(Jump.)*
And splashed all around.
(Put palms down; make splashing motions.)
The fishes swam away,
(Place hands together; wiggle.)
And didn't make a sound! *(Put fingers to lips.)*

Five Cranky Crabs

Author Unknown

Note: *Use name tags from page 39 as flannel board pieces with this fingerplay, or just hold up appropriate number of fingers.*

Five cranky crabs,
Were digging in the shore.
One swam into a net,
And now there were four.

Four cranky crabs,
Were floating off to sea.
One got tangled up in seaweed,
And now there were three.

Three cranky crabs,
Were wondering what to do.
One dug a deep, deep hole,
And now there were two.

Two cranky crabs,
Were warming in the sun.
One got scooped up in a cup,
And now there was one.

One cranky crab,
Was smarter than his friends.
He hid between the jagged rocks,
And that's how the story ends.

Activities

A Day at the Beach

Supplies needed:

- seashell macaroni
- paper
- glue
- cornmeal
- crayons/markers
- rubber stamps/ink pads
- construction paper scraps
- aluminum foil and colored saran pieces

Directions:

Have available an array of materials the children can use to create their own beach scene. Cornmeal makes great sand and the scraps can possibly be used to make fish or any sea creature they can imagine.

Windsurfing Boards

Supplies needed:

- scissors
- Styrofoam trays (clean vegetable or meat trays)
- tape
- markers/crayons
- Popsicle sticks
- paper 4¼" x 5½" (¼ sheet of paper)
- stickers, glitter glue, or colored glue *(optional)*

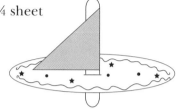

Directions:

1. Cut the Styrofoam tray into an oval shape.
2. Fold the paper in a triangle, taking the bottom left corner and bringing it up along the top edge of the paper (it will not match equally).
3. With the wide side facing down, place the Popsicle stick halfway up the paper and fold the extra edge over the stick two times.
4. Tape the backside, affixing the stick to the paper. You should now have a triangle that looks like a sail.
5. Stick the Popsicle stick into the Styrofoam.
6. Decorate your sail and board and you're ready to set sail!

Decorative Beachwear

Supplies needed:

- inexpensive flip-flops
- inexpensive sunglasses
- puffy paint (see recipe below)
- jewel beads
- glue
- glitter glue

Directions:

1. Allow the children to decorate the beach-wear you give them using the items listed above.

2. Allow their creativity to flow, but remind them to remember how the glasses and flip-flops are worn to determine where their designs should go.

3. Allow drying time before the children can wear or take the items home.

Puffy Paint Recipe

Supplies needed:

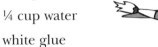

- ¼ cup flour
- ¼ cup salt
- ¼ cup water
- white glue
- colorant (food coloring may work, but professional cake decorating colorant works best)
- ¼ tsp alum (as a preservative)

Directions:

1. Mix the flour, salt, alum, and water together.

2. Add enough glue to colorant to give it a grainy, batter-type consistency.

3. Put the paint in a ziplock bag (cut the bottom tip to squeeze out), a small squeeze bottle (clean, empty condiment bottles work), or freezer paper wrapped in a cone.

4. Remember, the thicker the amount used, the longer it will take to dry.

Gross Motor Activities

Charlie Tuna

Have the children stand in a circle holding hands. Their arms go up and in and down and back (like fishing nets being cast into the sea), as they sing to the tune of "London Bridges."

Charlie tuna swims around,
Swims around,
Swims around.
Charlie tuna swims around,
Through the sea.

We shall cast our nets to fish,
Nets to fish,
Nets to fish.
We shall cast our nets to fish,
In the sea.

One child is chosen to be "Charlie." That child weaves in and out of the circle of children bringing their arms up and down. If "Charlie" gets caught in the downward arm motion of the children, he or she is caught and another child becomes "Charlie."

Swimming

Directions:

1. Everyone lies down on the floor on their stomachs. Have adequate room between children so no one touches.

2. Sing the song below as the children move their arms and legs as if swimming.

3. If you are not comfortable singing, use soothing music or ocean wave sounds.

4. Tell the children that when the singing or music stops, they can just "float" (stop moving).

5. If you wish you can sing faster or slower and have the children move accordingly.

Sung to the tune: "Twinkle, Twinkle, Little Star"

Swimming, swimming, out from shore,
Swimming, swimming, a bit more.
Move your arms and kick your feet,
Swimming with the fish is neat!
Keep on moving happily,
Through the water of the sea.

Math & Science Activities

From noses to Tails, Lengths, and Scales

Supplies needed:

- bathroom scale
- kitchen or food scale
- yarn or masking tape
- tape measure
- pictures and information on fishes and mammals of the sea found in books, encyclopedias, and the Internet
- index cards
- tape

Directions:

1. Look up the lengths and weights of various fish and mammals from the sea, such as whales, puffer fish, sharks, and clownfish.

2. List the weight of the sea fish and mammals you chose on index cards.

3. Weigh the children and chart their weight.

4. Have the children tape the index cards with the weight of the fish or mammal closest to their weight next to their name on the chart.

5. For those fish that weigh less than the children, see if you can find items within the room that weigh near the amount of the fish.

6. Weigh those items on the food or kitchen scale.

7. Measure the height of the children.

8. Using tape or yarn, lay out the length of some or all of the children on the floor.

9. Then measure and mark out the length of a whale, shark, and other fish.

10. Compare the lengths. Ask questions such as, "Which one is the longest?" "How much bigger is (child's name) than the (fish name)?" You may wish to have several children lay down end-to-end to see how many it would take to be the length of a whale, for example.

Fine Motor Skills Activity

Sand & Water Play

Supplies needed:

- dishpan
- sand
- water
- towels
- large trash bag
- measuring cups
- spoons
- cookie cutters

Directions:

1. Lay the trash bag down under the dishpan.

2. Add sand and enough water to dampen the sand and make it easier to clump together and clean up.

3. Give the children the measuring cups, spoons, and cookie cutters and allow them to have fun at the beach! (The towels are for clean up.)

Storytime Books to Share

Angel Fish by Iain Smyth. Piggy Toes Press, 2002. Angel Fish is searching for her mom. As she swims through the coral reef she encounters many ocean creatures. A pull and lift book.

Beach Babble by Kimberly Knutson. Marshall Cavendish, 1998. Three children enjoy the sounds and sights of a day at the ocean.

Beach Day! by Patricia Lakin. Dial, 2004. Four friends have many adventures on the way to the beach.

Beach Is to Fun: A Book of Relationships by Pat Brisson. Henry Holt & Company, 2004. A trip to the beach—and all the excitement that surrounds it—unfolds in this cheerful picture book chock-full of engaging wordplay and sensory detail. The rhythmic text explores the concept of analogies in an accessible, immediate way. Children can begin to make their own associations and pairings as they long for a day by the sea!

Beach Party! by Harriet Ziefert and Simms Taback. Blue Apple Books, 2005. Scooting! Sliding! Twisting! Trekking! Watch the animals parade across the sand, each in their own special way.

Bear's Adventure by Benedict Blathwayt. Knopf, 1988. A teddy bear left on the beach is swept out to sea and discovers the wonders on the ocean floor before being returned where he belongs.

Big Al and Shrimpy by Andrew Clements and Yoshi. Simon & Schuster, 2002. Shrimpy learns that even though he may be small, he can still make a big difference to his friend Big Al.

Clifford Keeps Cool by Norman Bridwell. Scholastic, 1999. During a long hot summer, Clifford tries many things to keep cool.

D. W. All Wet by Marc Brown. Little, Brown and Company, 1988. D. W. bosses her brother Arthur into carrying her on his shoulders at the beach because she maintains that she hates the water, until she gets a big wet surprise.

Ebb and Flo and the Greedy Gulls by Jane Simmons. Margaret K. McElderry Books, 2000. Ebb and Flo and their friend Bird are enjoying a peaceful day at the beach—until Flo accuses Ebb of eating all the sandwiches. But Ebb didn't do it! Everyone is disappointed with Ebb, so she goes off by herself to sulk.

Fidgety Fish by Ruth Galloway. Tiger Tales, 2001. Sent out for a swim in the deep sea, Tiddler, a young fish that just can't keep still, sees many interesting creatures and one dark cave.

A Fish Out of Water by Helen Palmer. Random House, 1961. Comic pictures show how the fish rapidly outgrows its bowl, a vase, a cook pot, and a bathtub.

Fish Wish by Bob Barner. Holiday House, 2000. A young boy's dream sends him on an underwater journey through a coral reef. Includes factual information on coral reefs and the animals that live in them.

Going to the Beach by Jo S. Kittinger. Children's Press, 2002. A family spends the day at the beach enjoying the water, sand, and sun.

Hello Ocean by Pam Muñoz Ryan. Talewinds, 2001. Using rhyming text, a child describes the wonder of the ocean experience through each of her five senses.

A House for Hermit Crab by Eric Carle. Picture Book Studio, 1987. A hermit crab that has outgrown his old shell moves into a new one, which he decorates and enhances with the various sea creatures he meets in his travels.

How Will We Get to the Beach? by Brigitte Luciani. North-South Books, 2000. One beautiful summer day, Roxanne decides to go to the beach. She loads up the car with everything she wants to take with her: the turtle, the umbrella, the book of wonderful stories, the ball, and of course, her baby. But the car won't start. Undaunted, Roxanne decides to take the bus to the beach. But something can't go on the bus. Whenever Roxanne comes up with a new way to get to the beach, she discovers she must leave something behind—and children will have great fun guessing just what's missing each time.

I Saw the Sea and the Sea Saw Me by Megan Montague Cash. Viking, 2001. A girl enjoys using all of her five senses to explore the ocean, but when a jellyfish appears she discovers that the sea is not always nice.

Let's Go Swimming with Mr. Sillypants by M. K. Brown. Crown Publishing, 1986. Mr. Sillypants worries so much about his swimming lesson that he has a dream in which he turns into a fish.

Little Fish Lost by Nancy Van Laan. Atheneum, 1998. Little Fish loses his mother in an African pond and searches everywhere for her, seeing all kinds of animals in the process.

The Mermaids' Lullaby by Kate Spohn. Random House, 1998. Mer-mommies and mer-daddies put their babies to sleep beneath the sea.

Mister Seahorse by Eric Carle. Philomel Books, 2004. After Mrs. Seahorse lays her eggs on Mr. Seahorse's belly, he drifts through the water greeting other fish fathers who are taking care of their eggs.

Moonbathing by Liz Rosenberg. Harcourt Brace, 1996. A young girl relishes the magical atmosphere of the beach at night when she goes for a moonlit stroll with her older cousin.

Night of the Moonjellies by Mark Shasha. Simon & Schuster, 1992. Seven-year-old Mark helps his grandmother and other family members run their seaside hot dog stand and then has a surprise at the end of the day.

Octopus Under the Sea by Connie and Peter Roop. Cartwheel, 2001. Basic factual information is told as an octopus goes through the sea.

Old Shell, New Shell by Helen Ward. Millbrook Press, 2002. A hermit crab who has outgrown his shell searches for a new one among the creatures of Australia's Great Barrier Reef. Includes a key which identifies the coral reef animals in the brightly colored and beautiful illustrations.

One Lonely Seahorse by Saxton Freymann and Joost Elffers. Arthur A. Levine, 2000. Go on an underwater jaunt with brilliant pictures of banana octopi, angelfish peppers, and more incredible fruit and vegetable sculptures that redefine the meaning of the word "seafood."

Paddington at the Seaside by Michael Bond. Random House, 1978. Paddington Bear's visit to the beach takes a comic turn when he innocently interrupts a Punch and Judy show.

Patrick and Ted at the Beach by Geoffrey Hayes. Random House, 1987. Patrick and his best friend Ted spend a fun-filled day at the beach.

The Pop-Up Commotion in the Ocean by Giles Andreae. Tiger Tales, 2002. Bright and colorful pop-ups bring to life sharks, angelfish, whales, penguins, and octopus.

Rainbow Fish and the Big Blue Whale by Marcus Pfister. North-South Books, 1998. Rainbow Fish and his friends enjoy eating the krill, or tiny shrimp, that populate the ocean floor. When a big whale comes into the area, he starts eating krill, too. Soon the fish worry that he'll eat them, and they hide when he's around. The hurt whale pretends that is just what he's going to do, but in the end, Rainbow Fish and the whale have a laugh over the misunderstanding, and everything works out fine.

Sand Cake by Frank Asch. Parents Magazine Press, 1978. Papa Bear uses his culinary skills and a little imagination to concoct a sand cake.

Sand in My Shoes by Wendy Kesselman. Hyperion Books for Children, 1995. A young girl regretfully says goodbye to her beach house, the seashore, and the summer as she prepares to return to the city.

Secret Seahorse by Stella Blackstone. Barefoot Books, 2004. A fish excitedly spots a seahorse, but can't keep up with the swift-moving creature. It searches the reef, swimming past stingrays, sharks, crabs, starfish, and a mermaid—until it finds a secret surprise.

Shamu and the Adventurous Seal Pup by Mark Shulman. SeaWorld Publications, 2002. When a baby seal pup goes out for adventure, Mama Seal calls to Shamu to help.

Ship by Chris L. Demarest. Red Wagon Books, 1995. Simple words and bright pictures describe a ship at sea.

Sink or Swim by Valerie Coulman. Lobster Press, 2003. Though everyone tells him cows don't swim, Ralph is determined to beat the heat.

Sun Dance, Water Dance by Jonathan London. Dutton Children's Books, 2001. An ode to summer with a group of friends spending a carefree day enjoying the great outdoors, plunging into snowmelt water after baking in the sun, walking barefoot, having picnics in the shade of a willow tree, and sleeping out under the stars.

Swim for Cover! Adventure on the Coral Reef by Sue Vyner. Crown Publishers, 1995. An octopus warns other sea creatures of a nearby predator on Australia's Great Barrier Reef. Includes brief information telling how each animal defends itself.

Swimmy by Leo Lionni. Pantheon, 1963. A little black fish in a school of red fish figures out a way of protecting them all from their natural enemies.

Ten Little Fish by Audrey Wood. Blue Sky Press, 2004. Told in playful verse with bright, colorful illustrations, this underwater tale counts ten little fish as they explore the ocean and swim through a sea filled with surprise and adventure.

There Was an Old Lady Who Swallowed a Trout! by Teri Sloat. Henry Holt & Company, 1998. Set on the coast of the Pacific Northwest, this variation on the traditional rhyme describes the silly consequences of an old woman's fishy diet.

Turtle in the Sea by Jim Arnosky. Putnam, 2002. A turtle emerges from the sea to lay her eggs in the sand.

Whales Passing by Eve Bunting. Blue Sky Press, 2003. A boy standing with his father on the shore watches five Orca whales and imagines them talking underwater in their star-dance light while the bubbles bubble up.

Who Lives in the Sea? by Alice Low. Marvel Books, 1987. Timmy and Penny are at the shore. See what they find when they explore the sea in this rhyming book.

Name Tag Patterns for Beach Days

Name Tag Patterns for Beach Days

Name Tag Patterns for Beach Days

Down On the Farm
Crops & Cattle, Farmers, Farm Animals & Tractors

Before Storytime

Name Tags

Copy the name tags on pages 50–51. Make enough copies so you have one name tag per child; cut out and list each child's name. You may wish to pin each name tag on with a safety pin, copy the name tags onto removable adhesive paper, or punch a hole in the top of each name tag and string it with yarn for a necklace.

Props

Ask at feed mills and tractor dealers if you can borrow a tractor or grain logo hat (a straw gardening hat would also be appropriate). Wear overalls and a shirt with rolled up sleeves and a bandanna in the pocket. Carry a basket of plastic vegetables or fruit, or show grains (oatmeal, rice, flour) and straw.

Storytime

- Introduce the theme by asking the children about their name tags.

- Show props and ask questions such as, "Who am I pretending to be?" "As a farmer, could I grow these foods?" "What foods do I have?" "Do you eat these foods?" "Do they look like this when you eat them?" "If you were a farmer, would you have animals? Which ones?" "What plants would you grow?" "Can you tell by my outfit what kind of farmer I would be?"

- Sing the storytime song on page 10.

- Intersperse stories, songs, fingerplays, and activities that fit within your time frame.

Snack

Edible Tractors

Supplies needed:

- hard boiled eggs
- cheese slices
- saltine crackers
- celery stalks (preferably with leaves on)
- plates

Directions:

1. Cook eggs until they are hard-boiled.
2. Slice eggs into circles.
3. On each child's plate, place a cracker for the front end of the tractor.
4. On the right side of the cracker, place a slice of cheese that is bigger than the cracker (pre-packaged cheese slices work best); this becomes the tractor cab.
5. Place four egg slices under the cheese slice for the wheels.
6. Behind the cheese slice, lay two celery stalks with the leaves on. This represents the plow.
7. Discuss that everything they are eating is grown on a farm. The crackers are made from wheat, etc.
8. Ask questions like, "Where do the eggs come from?" "Where does celery grow?" "Do you know what they need to do to the wheat to make it into a cracker?"

Discussion Questions

Ask specific questions to reinforce comprehension concepts, re-ignite excitement for the stories shared, enrich children's vocabulary, and influence narrative skills.

For example:

- "Who are some of the animals the little girl in *Sitting on the Farm* called to help?"
- "Name some of the animals mentioned in *Barnyard Banter*."
- "What animal was pictured for the letter "g" in *Farm Alphabet Book*?"
- "When spring arrived in *The Quiet Little Farm*, there were four of what animal?"
- "Tell me some of the things that happened in *This Is the Farmer*."
- "What were some of the cow's demands in *Click, Clack, Moo: Cows That Type*?"
- "How do the animals chase away the farmer in *Farmer Duck*?"

Wrapping It Up

Sing the song on page 11.

Songs

Cows Give Milk

Sung to the tune: "All Around the Mulberry Bush"

Cows give milk, yes they do,
Yes they do, yes they do.

Cows give milk we love to drink,
Yum, yum, yum!

Milk is used to make us cheese,
Ice cream, too, and yogurt—oooh!

So many treats we love to eat,
Come from cow's milk.

Farm Animals

What animals live on a farm?
What animals live on a farm?
What animals live on a farm?

(Child's name), can you name one?
(Name what the child says, singing.)
A _____ lives on a farm, yes it does,
A _____ lives on a farm, yes it does,
A _____ lives on a farm, yes it does,
And it says _____. *(Make that animal's sound, repeat sound three times.)*

Farm Workers

Sung to the tune: "Row, Row, Row Your Boat"

I'm a worker on a farm.
Riding on a tractor.
Plowing, working all the day,
Help crops grow the right way.

I'm a worker on a farm.
I work hard all through the day.
But it's worth it when I see
The crops growing happily!

Down at the Farmyard

Author Unknown

Sung to the tune: "Down by the Station"

Down at the farmyard,
Early in the morning.
See the little tractor,
Standing in the barn.

Do you hear the farmer,
Start the tractor's engine?
Chug, chug, vroom, vroom,
Off he goes!

The Fly

Author Unknown

Sung to the tune: "Farmer in the Dell"

A fly is on my nose,
A fly is on my nose,
Hi-ho! And buzz, buzz, buzz,
A fly is on my nose.

The fly is on a cow,
It's swishing its tail right now,
Hi-ho! The dairy-o!
The fly is on a cow.

The fly is on a pig,
It's rolling and doing a jig!
Hi-ho! And buzz, buzz, buzz,
The fly is on a pig.

The fly is on a horse,
He's bothered by it of course!
Hi-ho! And buzz, buzz, buzz,
The fly is on a horse.

The fly went by my cat,
She swatted and she spat.
Hi-ho! And buzz, buzz, buzz,
The fly went by my cat.

The fly went by my mat,
And I went ... SPLAT!
Hi-ho! The dairy-o!
The fly went SPLAT!

Baa-Baa Black Sheep

Traditional

Baa, baa, black sheep,
Have you any wool?
Yes sir, yes sir,
Three bags full;

One for the master,
And one for the dame,
And one for the little boy,
Who lives down the lane.

Action Songs

Farm Chores

Author Unknown

Sung to the tune: "All Around the Mulberry Bush"

(Act out each job on the farm.)

This is the way we feed the chicks,
Feed the chicks, feed the chicks.
This is the way we feed the chicks,
So early in the morning.

This is the way we hoe the field,
Hoe the field, hoe the field.
This is the way we hoe the field,
So early in the morning.

Other options:

Plant the seeds.
Pull the weeds.
Milk the cows.
Brush the horse.
Shear the sheep.

I'm a Little Piggy

Sung to the tune: "I'm a Little Teapot"

I'm a little piggy,
(Point to self or tickle child on lap.)
Short and stout. *(Standing, bend at knees.)*
Here are my ears, *(Point to ears.)*
And here is my snout. *(Point to nose.)*

When I'm in the pigpen, *(Do knee bends as you
encircle yourself with your arms.)*
I eat from a pail. *(Pretend to eat with hands
under your face in a circle.)*

I say oink, oink, *(Make "oink" sounds.)*
And I wiggle my tail. *(Shake back end like wiggling a tail.)*

Working on the Farm

Author Unknown

Sung to the tune: "All Around the Mulberry Bush"

We are working on the farm,
(Pretend to hoe a field.)
On the farm, on the farm.
We are working on the farm,
It's hard work, but it's worth it! *(Wipe brow.)*

This is the way we feed the cows,
(Pretend to feed the cows.)
Feed the cows, feed the cows,
This is the way we feed the cows,
It's hard work, but it's worth it! *(Wipe brow.)*

Continue with: ride the horse, plant the corn,
gather the eggs, pet the cats, etc.

Ask the children for other suggestions. Act
out the words as you sing along.

Fingerplays

Five Little Chicks

Five little chicks about to hatch,
(Hold up five fingers.)
The first one took out a little patch.
(Wiggle thumb.)
The second one asked if they all matched.
(Wiggle pointer finger.)
The third one had a big black patch.
(Wiggle middle finger.)
The fourth one was as sleepy as can be,
(Wiggle ring finger.)
And the fifth one just cheeped with glee!
(Wiggle pinky finger.)

This Little Calf

Author Unknown

This little calf eats grass.
(Hold up five fingers; push one down at a time.)
This little calf eats hay.
This little calf drinks water.
This little calf runs away.
This little calf does nothing,
But just lies down all day.
(Rest last finger in palm of other hand.)

Five Pink Pigs

Five pink pigs in the farm pen.
(Hold up five fingers.)
The first one ate next to the hen.
(Wiggle thumb.)
The second one went to eat again, and again.
(Wiggle index finger.)
The third one was shoved away before he was
done. *(Wiggle middle finger.)*
The fourth one just liked to have fun.
(Wiggle ring finger.)
The fifth one, he was big and fat,
*(Wiggle pinky; place hands out wide at the
side of your body.)*
He sat on the farmer's hat!
(Cover mouth with shocked expression on face.)

Here is a Barn

Author Unknown

Here is a barn so big as you see.
*(Use hands to draw a roof and sides of barn in the
air; spread arms out wide, point to children, and
place hand over eyes.)*

In walk the milking cows,
(Walk fingers; make "moo" sound.)

One, two, three.
(Hold up three fingers, one at a time.)

Soon there'll be milk for you and me!
(Point to children, then self.)

Activities

Who's in the Barn?

Supplies needed:

* barn name tag on page 51
* crayons/markers
* cotton balls (1 per child)
* fine-point red permanent marker
* glue
* construction paper, small amount of black and one other color
* scissors
* tape
* hole punch

Directions:

1. Copy and enlarge the barn name tag to a full-sized sheet (8½" x 11").

2. Cut the barn door with scissors so it hinges open.

3. Tape a square of construction paper behind the barn door (just large enough to cover the door with a bit extra around the sides).

4. Have the children color their barn.

5. Give each child a cotton ball and have them glue it behind the barn door on the construction paper.

6. Using a crayon or marker, have the children give the "sheep" legs.

7. Use a permanent marker to draw a face on the sheep.

8. Have the children punch out one circle from the black construction paper and cut it in half.

9. Glue these half circles on for the sheep's ears.

Edible Art

Ice Cream in a Bag

Courtesy of Wisconsin Milk Marketing Board

Ingredients Needed:

* ½ cup heavy whipping cream
* 1 tsp sugar
* ¼ tsp vanilla
* 1 sandwich-sized freezer-safe ziplock bag
* 1 large bag
* crushed ice
* rock or kosher salt
* oven mitts

Directions:

1. In a small bowl, combine cream, sugar, and vanilla.

2. Pour the mixture into the sandwich-sized bag. Seal tightly, squeezing out as much air as possible.

3. Place the small sealed bag inside the larger bag. Fill the outside of the bag

three quarters of the way with crushed ice. Sprinkle rock or kosher salt over ice and seal the bag tightly, again squeezing out as much air as possible.

4. Have the children shake the bag. Give them an oven mitt to wear so that their hands won't get cold.

5. As the children shake, talk with them about what's going on. Ask, "Does it look like ice cream yet?" "No, why?" "What does it look like?"

6. Encourage the use of descriptive words and try to relate what they see to things seen before. For example, "It looks like milk. Now it's getting thicker. It feels like pudding."

7. After 5 to 10 minutes of continuous shaking, the ice cream should be frozen and ready to eat!

Gross Motor Activity

Off to the Farm

Directions:

1. Gather all of the children in a circle.

2. As you hold hands and circle round, sing the song below to the tune of "The Farmer in the Dell":

   We're off to the farm,
   We're off to the farm.
   Hee-haw, here's what I saw,
   While off on the farm.

3. Name one child to go in the center of the circle.

4. Everyone stops walking and stands in a circle around the child.

5. The child in the center pretends to be something on a farm, such as a cow, pig, cat, horse, goat, tractor, farmer in the garden, dog, sheep, etc., by acting and sounding out the one thing he or she has chosen.

6. Everyone standing in the circle guesses what he or she is pretending to be.

7. The first child who correctly identifies what he or she is acting out is next to be inside the circle.

Math & Science Activity

Sour Milk

Supplies needed:

- 2 tablespoons milk
- 1 tsp white vinegar in a glass
- 1 tsp water in a glass
- 2 small dishes
- spoon

Directions:

1. Place 1 tablespoon of milk in each small dish.

2. Discuss what milk is, how we use it, and where it comes from.

3. Show the glasses of water and vinegar. Ask the children if they look the same. Have them smell each of them. Do they recognize the smell? Does anyone know what it is? What do they think will happen when you add the water and vinegar to the milk?

4. Pour the water in one dish of milk and the vinegar in the other.

5. Stir. Let stand for about 5 minutes.

6. As you wait, talk to the children about sour or spoiled milk. Have they ever had a time when they drank milk and it tasted funny? Inside the cow's body, milk is always at the right temperature, but once we take the milk from the cow it needs to be kept cold so bacteria will not spoil (or sour) it. Bacteria change the look and taste of the milk.

7. Look in the two dishes. Spoon out some of the milk from the vinegar dish and ask the children if it looks like milk they would want to drink.

8. Show them the other dish and discuss what has happened.

9. Explain you used water in that dish. Talk about how that changed the milk. Ask, "Would that milk be safe to drink?"

10. Enjoy a nice, cold glass of milk.

11. Some of your more curious children might ask, "Why is it all right to have warm milk before bed?" Clarify that heating it on a stove is safe because it heats quicker than bacteria can form. We added something to the milk to make it sour quickly.

Fine Motor Skills Activity

Seed Sort

Supplies needed:

- many packages of various seeds, including flowers and vegetables *

- large cookie sheet with sides (jelly roll pans)

- tape or glue

Directions:

1. Place the seed packets out and have the children sort them according to category (flowers or vegetables).

2. Tape or glue one seed from inside each package to the outside.

3. Open the packages and have the children sort the seeds according to color, shape, and size.

4. Have the children place the seeds back in the correct package by matching the seed that is attached to the front.

   * Purchasing out-of-date seeds saves a lot of money, and some stores may even donate them to your school or library.

Storytime Books to Share

Baa Baa Black Sheep told by Iza Trapani. Whispering Coyote Books, 2001. In this expanded version of the traditional nursery rhyme, the black sheep has a surprise for the other farm animals.

Barn Dance by Bill Martin Jr. and John Archambault. Henry Holt & Company, 1986. Unable to sleep on the night of a full moon, a young boy follows the sound of music across the fields and finds an unusual barn dance in progress.

Barn Sneeze by Karen B. Winnick. Boyds Mills Press, 2002. None of the animals in Sue's barn can stop sneezing.

Barnyard Banter by Denise Fleming. Henry Holt & Company, 1994. All the farm animals are where they should be, clucking and mucking, mewing and cooing, except for the missing goose.

Barnyard Boogie by Jim and Janet Post. Accord Publishing, 2002. Various farm animals introduce themselves and sing their respective animal sounds. Includes die-cut pages, which allow the reader to use an attached hand puppet to accompany them.

Barnyard Dance by Sandra Boynton. Workman Publishing, 1993. A board book featuring a bespectacled fiddle-playing cow and a pig twirling a sheep gets everyone to do a barnyard dance.

Barnyard Lullaby by Frank Asch. Simon & Schuster, 1998. Although the farmer only hears animal noises, when the different barnyard animals sing lullabies to their respective children, the babies understand the words. Includes music.

Bear in the Barnyard by Sue Robinson. Good Books, 2004. Teddy Bear enjoys playing with a toy barnyard while everyone is asleep, but when he visits a real farm, a horse challenges him to find out what he can do to help out, as all of the farm animals do.

Big Red Barn by Margaret Wise Brown. HarperCollins, 1989. Rhymed text and illustrations introduce the many different animals that live in the big barn.

Can Roosters Sing in Tune? by Nancy Parent. Paradise Press, 2001. Animals of the barnyard share their tune in this rhyming board book.

Click, Clack, Moo: Cows That Type by Doreen Cronin. Simon & Schuster, 2000. When Farmer Brown's cows find a typewriter in the barn, they start making demands and go on strike when the farmer refuses to give them what they want.

Cornfield Hide-and-Seek by Christine Barker Widman. Melanie Kroupa Books, 2003. When the whole family is so hot that they hide in the cool cornfield, Mamaw decides to play along with a hide-and-seek game of her own.

Cows in the Kitchen by June Crebbin. Candlewick Press, 1998. While Tom Farmer is asleep under the haystack, the cows, ducks, pigs, hens, and sheep make quite a mess in the farmhouse.

Down on the Farm by Merrily Kutner. Holiday House, 2004. Simple rhyming text describes the sounds and activities of animals during a day on the farm.

Down on the Farm by Rita Lascaro. Harcourt Brace, 1999. A child naps like a cat, flaps like a hen, swims like a duck, and imitates the other animals on the farm.

Early Morning in the Barn by Nancy Tafuri. Greenwillow Books, 1983. All the barnyard animals wake up when the rooster crows.

Emma and the Coyote by Margriet Ruurs. Stoddart Kids, 1999. There's a hungry coyote on the prowl, and everyone is frightened. But not Emma—she thinks that chickens are smarter than coyotes and she intends to prove it.

Everything Is Different at Nonna's House by Caron Lee Cohen. Clarion Books, 2003. A young boy describes the differences between his home in the city and life on his grandparents' farm, learning that no matter where he is, their love for him is always the same.

Farm Alphabet Book by Jane Miller. Prentice Hall, 1983. Photographs of farm animals and objects, accompanied by simple descriptions, illustrate the letters of the alphabet.

Farmer Brown Goes Round and Round by Teri Sloat. DK Publishing, 1999. A twister strikes Farmer Brown's farm and mixes the animals all up, so that the cows oink, sheep cluck, hens bray, and his hound neighs.

Farmer Duck by Martin Waddell. Candlewick Press, 1992. When a kind and hardworking duck nearly collapses from overwork, while taking care of a farm because the owner is too lazy to do so, the rest of the animals get together and chase the farmer out of town.

Farmer McPeepers and His Missing Milk Cows by Katy Duffield. Rising Moon Press, 2003. A crafty herd of cows borrows Farmer McPeepers' eyeglasses so that they can have a day on the town.

The Farm Life by Elizabeth Spurr. Holiday House, 2003. Rhymed descriptions of life on a farm introduce basic colors and the numbers one to ten.

Farm Morning by David McPhail. Voyager Books, 1985. A father and his young daughter share a special morning as they feed all the animals on their farm.

Fiddle-i-Fee illustrated by Santiago Cohen. Blue Apple Books, 2003. "I had a hen and the hen pleased me, and I fed my hen under the yonder tree ..." And so goes the traditional song illustrated in bright colors and done in a rebus format.

The Flea's Sneeze by Lynn Downey. Henry Holt & Company, 2000. A flea with a cold startles all the animals in the barn when it sneezes unexpectedly.

Giggle, Giggle, Quack by Doreen Cronin. Simon & Schuster, 2002. When Farmer Brown goes on vacation, leaving his brother Bob in charge, Duck makes trouble by changing all the instructions to notes the animals like much better.

How to Speak Moo! by Deborah Fajerman. Barron's, 2002. Learn the high moo and the low moo, the bumpy moo and the jumpy moo. Discover how your moo sounds in a tunnel or through a funnel and other moo-velous places!

Let's Go Visiting by Sue Williams. Harcourt, 1998. Let's go visiting and see who's ready to play—one foal, two calves, three kittens, four piglets, five ducklings, and six puppies! And once we've stomped in the mud with the piglets and swum in the lake with the ducklings, let's curl up with this adorable menagerie and take an afternoon nap.

Maisy at the Farm by Lucy Cousins. Candlewick Press, 1998. Lift the flaps and see Maisy do all kinds of chores on the farm. A Parenting Reading Magic Award Winner as well as an Oppenheim Toy Gold Seal Award Winner.

Maisy's Morning on the Farm by Lucy Cousins. Candlewick Press, 2001. Morning is a busy time on the farm and Maisy needs to feed the animals before she can eat.

The Midnight Farm by Reeve Lindbergh. Dial, 1987. Secrets of the dark are revealed in this poem describing a farm at midnight.

Mrs. Mooley by Jack Kent. Golden Books, 2002. Inspired by a picture in the nursery rhyme book left on the barn floor, Mrs. Mooley, the cow, is determined to jump over the moon, despite the ridicule of the other barnyard animals.

Mrs. Wishy-Washy's Farm by Joy Cowley. Philomel Books, 2003. Tired of being washed by Mrs. Wishy-Washy, a cow, pig, and duck leave her farm and head for the city.

Noisy Barn by Harriet Ziefert. Blue Apple Books, 2003. A boisterous parade of farm animals on their way to the barn certainly can cause quite a stir. With the cow mooing, the piglet oinking, the duck quacking, the chickens pecking, and the cat meowing, it's a wonder they arrive at all.

The Noisy Farm: Lots of Animal Noises to Enjoy! by Marni McGee. Bloomsbury Children's Books, 2004. A farmer goes through his daily activities on the farm, accompanied by the sounds of animals and other things.

Oh, Crumps! by Lee Bock. Raven Tree Press, 2003. The misadventures of a sleepy farmer as he agonizes over a mixed-up list of the coming day's chores. How will he ever milk the fence, repair the cow, mow the silo, and climb the hay before morning comes? Text in English and Spanish.

Old MacDonald Had a Barn by Stephen Gulbis. Chrysalis Books, 2003. Old MacDonald had a ... barn? Based on the traditional nursery rhyme, *Old MacDonald Had a Barn* is an interactive book with a brilliant pop-up twist! Find out why all of the animals are fleeing the barn with this much-loved rhyme, complete with a surprise ending.

Old MacDonald Had a Farm by Penny Dann. Orchard Books, 1998. Colorful illustrations to the traditional song.

Peek-A-Boo Guess Who Farm Animals by Salina Yoon. Piggy Toes Press, 2002. Each page has text clues and lift-the-flap panels for a variety of animals.

Peek-a-Moo by Marie Torres Cimarusti. Dutton Children's Books, 1998. Play peek-a-boo with bright, quirky animals on each page, guess what they are, then lift the flap to find out.

Pete and Polo's Farmyard Adventure by Adrian Reynolds. Orchard Books, 2001. When Pete and his polar bear, Polo, visit Grandpa on his farm, they help him find ten missing ducklings.

Pigs in the House by Steven Kroll. Parents Magazine Press, 1983. When three cute pigs get into the farmhouse, total chaos results.

The Quiet Little Farm by Janet Kerr. Henry Holt & Company, 2000. As winter turns to spring, young farm animals come outdoors to play.

Rooster Can't Cock-a-Doodle-Doo by Karen Rostoker-Gruber. Dial, 2004. When Rooster's throat is too sore for him to crow, the other farm animals help both him and Farmer Ted.

Sitting on the Farm by Bob King. Orchard Books, 1992. A girl trying to get a bug off her knee enlists the aid of a series of increasingly larger animals.

Snappy Little Farmyard by Dugald Steer. Silver Dolphin, 2002. Bold bright graphics, a simple clean design, engaging rhyming text that appeals to young kids, and big pop-ups on each spread; a day on the farm has never been quite so much fun—or quite so noisy— thanks to this mooing, baaing, and neighing menagerie.

Spot Goes to the Farm by Eric Hill. Putnam, 1987. Spot visits a farm where his dad drives a tractor and he looks for baby animals. A lift-the-flap book.

This Farm Is a Mess by Leslie McGuire. Dutton Children's Books, 1981. Unable to stand the mess on Farmer Wood's farm any longer, the animals decide to do something about it.

This Is the Farmer by Nancy Tafuri. Greenwillow Books, 1994. A farmer's kiss causes an amusing chain of events on the farm.

Two Crazy Pigs by Karen Berman Nagel. Cartwheel, 1992. Two pigs who drive the farmer and his wife crazy with their silliness and pranks decide to move to a new farm, only to be missed by all the other animals when they leave.

What's that Awful Smell? by Heather Tekavec. Dial, 2004. While investigating an odor in their barn, a group of animals discovers a little piglet and engages in a variety of antics to get rid of the awful smell.

When the Cows Come Home by David Harrison. Boyds Mills Press, 1994. A herd of cows ride bicycles, square dance, go swimming, and more in this rhyming picture book.

Who's Knocking at the Door? by Carla Stevens. Marshall Cavendish, 2004. An elderly farm couple gives shelter to a talking horse, a cow, and two hens on a cold night. In gratitude, the animals save them from two robbers.

Who's On the Farm? by Heather J. Gondek. Piggy Toes Press, 2001. This engaging lift-the-flap book will help beginning readers get comfortable with the reading process by helping them recognize important first words. Lively sentences are composed of words and pictures. Lift the picture flaps and see the matching words underneath, then add up the clues—young ones will love the challenge of figuring out what friendly farm animal is hidden under the giant lift-flap on each page.

Who Wakes Rooster? by Clare Hodgson Meeker. Simon & Schuster, 1996. The animals on the farm stay asleep until the sun rouses the rooster, whose crowing wakes up everyone else.

Z-Z-Zoink! by Bernard Most. Harcourt Brace, 1999. A pig has trouble finding a place to sleep because she snores so loudly and wakes up the entire barnyard.

Name Tag Patterns for Down On the Farm

Name Tag Patterns for Down On the Farm

Fun Under the Big Top
Circus

Before Storytime

Name Tags

Copy the name tags on pages 60–62. Make enough copies so you have one name tag per child; cut out and list each child's name. You may wish to pin each name tag on with a safety pin, copy onto removable adhesive paper, or punch a hole in the top of each name tag and string it with yarn for a necklace.

Props

- Wear silly clothes, face paint (see recipe on page 56), and dress like a clown.

- Borrow a tuxedo coat (you can also check resale shops) and wear a top hat (make one from cardboard and black construction paper) to be a ringmaster.

- If you are brave, wear leotards and be a trapeze artist.

- Wear a leopard print or tiger-striped shirt (check yard sales or resale shops), along with boots and a pretend whip, to be a lion tamer. Carry a stuffed lion for added effect.

Storytime

- Introduce the theme by asking the children about their name tags.

- Show props and ask questions such as, "Would you like to be a clown?" "Seeing how I am dressed, what should my clown name be?" "What does a ringmaster do?" "Do you think I'm in danger of this lion, as its tamer?"

- Sing the storytime song on page 10.

- Intersperse stories, songs, fingerplays, and activities that fit within your time frame.

Snack

Serve lemonade, popcorn, and apples on a stick (place a small apple on a Popsicle stick).

Discussion Questions

Ask specific questions to reinforce comprehension concepts, re-ignite excitement for the stories shared, enrich children's vocabulary, and influence narrative skills.

For example:

- "What was wrong with everyone that Olivia had to save the circus in *Olivia Saves the Circus*?"

- "Where are some of the places the clown looks for his pup in the book *Where's Pup*?"

- "Tell me some of the things you remember seeing in the book *Last Night I Dreamed a Circus*."

- "What are some of the things they did to plan a circus in *Miss Bindergarten Plans a Circus with Kindergarten*?"

- "Name some of the things Sara did to practice in *Sara Joins the Circus*."

- "Where did the men who stopped to help Curious George with his bike take him?" "What did the ostrich eat in the book *Curious George Rides a Bike*?"

Wrapping It Up

Sing the song on page 11.

Songs

Circus Song

Author Unknown

Sung to the tune: "I've Been Working on the Railroad"

I am walking through the circus,
Happy as can be.

I am walking through the circus,
Just to see what I can see.

I can see the clown laughing.
I can see the elephants, too.

I can see the lion sleeping,
Look out, he sees you too!

Circus Elephants

Sung to the tune: "The Ants Go Marching"

Elephants walk in circus rings, *(Walk like an elephant.)*
They swing and sway. *(Hold arms like an elephant trunk and swing.)*
Elephant's trunks hold onto tails,
They walk this way. *(Walk like an elephant.)*

The elephants in the circus ring,
They work and play, they're a funny thing,
To see perform in the circus ring.
They swing and sway, *(Hold arms like an elephant trunk and swing.)*
And walk this way. *(Walk like an elephant.)*

Funny Clown

Author Unknown

Sung to the tune: "Teddy Bear, Teddy Bear, Turn Around"

Funny clown, funny clown,
Spin around.

Funny clown, funny clown,
Jump up and down.

Funny clown, funny clown,
Touch your toes.

Funny clown, funny clown,
Honk your nose!

We Are Clowns Today

Sung to the tune: "The Farmer in the Dell"

We are clowns today,
Let's smile and shout hooray!
Wow-whee! What do you say?
We are clowns today!

Additional verses: We'll do tricks today. We'll be goofy all day. We'll make you laugh today.

I'm an Acrobat

Sung to the tune: "Frére Jacques"

I'm an acrobat, I'm an acrobat.
Watch me fly, fly so high.
Watch me twirl and watch me spin,
Way up high, then low again,
Come and see, then clap for me.

Fingerplays

Going to the Circus

Author Unknown

Going to the circus to have a lot of fun.
The animals parading, one by one.
(Hold up one finger on each hand.)

Now they're walking two by two,
(Hold up two fingers on each hand.)
A great big lion and a caribou.

Now they're walking three by three,
(Hold up three fingers on each hand.)
The elephants and the chimpanzee.

Now they're walking four by four,
(Hold up four fingers on each hand.)
A stripy tiger and a big old boar.

Now they're walking five by five,
(Hold up five fingers on each hand.)
Make us laugh when they arrive.

Now they're walking six by six,
(Hold up six fingers.)
Little dogs jump over sticks.

Now they're walking seven by seven,
(Hold up seven fingers.)
Zebras striped, I counted eleven.

Now they're walking eight by eight,
(Hold up eight fingers.)
Running and jumping over the gate.

Now they're walking nine by nine,
(Hold up nine fingers.)
Great big elephants and a porcupine.

Now they're walking ten by ten,
(Hold up ten fingers.)
Ready to parade all around again.

Wiggles the Clown

I wear a funny little hat.
I have a funny nose.
Sometimes I'm thin.
Sometimes I'm fat.
My shoes have floppy toes.
I wiggle, wiggle all about.
I jiggle up and down.
I make children laugh and shout.
It's fun to be a clown.

Acrobat

Author Unknown

One little acrobat swinging through the air,
(Hold index finger up and swing from side to side.)

He flips and flops as we stare. *(Make index finger bend up and down.)*

And suddenly, he's caught by another with flare! *(Show excitement; lock both index fingers together.)*

He didn't even know he gave me a scare!
(Shake head and wipe brow.)

One little acrobat swinging through the air,
(Hold index finger up and swing side to side.)

He lands and bows with the greatest of care!
(With left palm facing up, place right hand index finger up on left palm and bend it as to bow.)

Five Big Elephants

Author Unknown

Five big elephants—oh, what a sight! *(Hold up five fingers.)*

Swinging their trunks from left to right.
(Clasp both hands together and swing.)

Four are followers, and one is the king.
(Show four fingers on one hand and one finger on another.)

They all walk around the circus ring. *(Draw a circle with your index finger pointing to the ground.)*

Elephant

Author Unknown

An elephant goes like this and like that.
(Pat knees.)
He's terribly big and he's terribly fat.
(Put hands out wide.)
He has no fingers, *(Wiggle fingers.)*
He has no toes, *(Touch toes.)*
But goodness gracious, what a nose!
(Make curling movement away from nose.)

Activities

Clown Shoes

Supplies needed:

- small oatmeal boxes, approximately 7" in height—1 per child
- markers
- hole punch
- glitter glue
- pom-poms
- bric-a-brac
- scissors
- yarn—1 3-foot piece per child with one end taped

Directions:

1. Remove the label from the oatmeal container.

2. Remove the inner plastic ring.

3. Using the bottom of the container as the front of your clown shoe, cut from the top of the box approximately 1½" down the side, then curve down to the bottom. Do the same on the other side. This goes over the top of one of your shoes. Cut another oatmeal container to make the second shoe.

4. Using the hole punch, place two holes on either side of the cardboard, at the back of the shoe.

5. Have the children decorate their clown shoes.

6. Depending on your time frame and the age of the children, you may wish to either lace the holes or have them do it. This is a great opportunity to use con-

ceptual language as the "shoe" is being laced with the yarn. Begin by lacing up the right bottom hole, then down the left top hole, up the right top hole, and down the left bottom hole. Lacing in this fashion allows you to tie the "shoe" over the children's shoe and around their ankles.

Animal Circus Train

Supplies needed:

- copy the basic circus train pattern on page 63
- crayons/markers
- animal cookies *
- glue
- construction paper
- scissors

Directions:

1. Allow the children to color their circus train.

2. Give them pre-cut strips of construction paper or have them cut strips for the bars on the animal boxcar.

3. They may also wish to cover the wheels with construction paper or just color those on the paper.

4. Glue the animal cookies on the train car for a 3D effect.

5. Glue just the ends of the construction paper strips to the top and bottom of the train car, creating the bars to hold the circus animals in the boxcar.

   * You will need to have a "glue only" cookie pile and an edible cookie pile to avoid an unpleasant experience.

Gross Motor Activities

Did You Ever See a Clown?

Sung to the tune: "Did You Ever See a Lassie?"

Call on one child at a time to get in the center of the "circus ring" circle and make a funny face.

Sing:
> Did you ever see a clown?
> A clown, a clown,
> Did you ever see a clown,
> Make a silly face like that?

> Thank you Mr./Miss clown,
> We thank you, please sit down.
> Did you ever see a clown,
> Make a silly face like that?

Silly Pokey

Sung to the tune: "Hokey Pokey"

All stand in a circle and sing:

You put your clown feet in,
You put your clown feet out,
You put your clown feet in,
And you shake them all about.

You do the silly pokey,
And you turn yourself around,
That's how you clown around!

Additional verses: clown hair, clown face, silly self.

Clown, Clown, Ringmaster

Play a version of Duck, Duck, Goose using "clown" to replace duck, and "ringmaster" to replace goose.

Tightrope Walking

Supplies needed:

- clothesline
- balloon *(optional)*

Directions:

Place a clothesline on the ground and have the children pretend to be tightrope walkers. You may also add to the difficulty (and silliness) by having them walk the "tightrope" with a balloon between their knees.

Clown Dress Relay

Supplies needed:

- 4 bags
- old clothes
- old jewelry
- old shoes
- hats
- scarves

Directions:

1. Line the children up in two lines and place a bag of dress-up items in front of each line.

2. Set two empty bags at the opposite end of the room.

3. Two children, one at a time (the first in each line), dress in the clothes in the bag and move quickly to the other end of the room, where they take the items off and put them in that bag.

4. Continue until all in each line have had a turn.

Math & Science Activities

Silly, Shocking Hair

Supplies needed:

- balloon
- willing child with medium length hair (lighter, thinner hair works better than thick hair)

Directions:

1. Just for fun, rub a balloon on someone's hair, and watch it stand on end!

2. Explain that the air has things in it we cannot see. What they just saw were electrons working! Electrons are always there, but when the air is dry and we rub against them (rub hands together in opposite directions to demonstrate), they can shock us, like what we saw the hair do.

3. Ask if anyone has ever touched a doorknob after walking across carpet and has gotten a shock.

Number Toss

Supplies needed:

- beanbags
- box
- clown face or markers
- scissors or a retractable knife

Directions:

1. Cut holes in a box large enough for a beanbag to fit through with some extra room to spare.

2. Decorate the box with either a clown face or numbers by each hole. Encircle the middle hole with red for the clown's nose (bull's eye).

3. Have everyone count out loud the number of tosses each child makes.

4. If you have numbers on your box, say the number each child tosses it in, or next to, after they toss their beanbag.

Options:
Use coffee can lids with the centers cut out and place a small table upside down so the children can toss it over the legs of the upright table.

Count how many "ringers" the children get. You may even wish to add all the "ringers" up for a simple addition demonstration.

Face Paint Recipe

Supplies needed:

- 1 tsp corn starch
- ½ tsp water
- ½ tsp cold cream or solid vegetable shortening
- 2 drops food coloring

Directions:

Mix the above ingredients together, and blend well.

Fine Motor Skills Activities

Clown Juggling School

Supplies needed:

- 3 scarves
- 3 small foam balls
- 3 plastic deli container lids with centers cut out

Directions:

1. Demonstrate juggling with the various objects.

2. Allow the children to practice.

   Note: You may also wish to have books available for the children to look through, such as *Nick Huckleberry Beak's Awesome Juggling Tricks* by Nick Huckleberry (Southwater, 2001), *I Want to Be a Juggler* by Iva Bulloch (Thomson Learning, 1995), and *Juggling for the Complete Klutz* by John Cassidy (Klutz Press, 1994).

Circus Match

Supplies needed:

- name tags from pages 60–62
- markers, colored pencils, crayons

Directions:

1. Decorate the name tags so there are two alike in each design.

2. Decorate others that are the same shape, but with differences that the children can notice.

3. Have the children match the two that are the same.

4. Discuss the differences in the others. Ask, "Are they the same shape?" "How are they different?"

Storytime Books to Share

All Aboard the Circus Train! by Laura Driscoll. Simon Spotlight, 2004. Join Dora the Explorer and Boots as they find their way to the circus. A fold-out, lift-the-flap book.

The Amazing Love Story of Mr. Morf: An Astonishing Circus Romance by Carll Cneut. Clarion Books, 2003. Everyone around him seems happy being paired up, so Mr. Morf the circus dog sets off to find a special friend for himself.

Babar's Little Circus Star by Laurent de Brunhoff. Random House, 1988. Unhappy because she is the smallest in the family, Isabelle discovers that being little has its advantages when she is asked to perform in the circus.

Barnyard Big Top by Jill Kastner. Simon & Schuster, 1997. When Uncle Julius visits his sisters' farm and brings his Two-Ring Extravaganza along, he livens up everything.

Bearymore by Don Freeman. Viking, 1976. A circus bear has trouble hibernating and dreaming up a new act at the same time.

Circus by Lois Ehlert. HarperCollins, 1992. Leaping lizards, marching snakes, a bear on the high wire, and others perform in a somewhat unusual circus.

Circus by Brian Wildsmith. Millbrook Press, 1996. Full-page color illustrations capture the animals, clown, and acrobatic acts of the circus.

Circus Adventures by Lindsey Wolter. Landmark Editions, 1996. While at the circus, a girl suddenly becomes part of the show after being swooped up by the lady on the horse.

The Circus Alphabet by Linda Bronson. Henry Holt & Company, 2001. Simple rhyming text and illustrations present some aspect of the circus for each letter from A to Z.

Circus Caps for Sale by Esphyr Slobodkina. HarperCollins, 2002. A peddler who sells caps by balancing them all on his head is invited to do an act in the circus.

Circus Family Dog by Andrew Clements. Clarion Books, 2000. Grumps is content to do his one trick in the center ring at the circus, until a new dog shows up and steals the show—temporarily.

Circus Fun by Margaret Hillert. Follett Publishing, 1969. A boy and his father go to the circus and bring home something for his mother.

Circus Girl by Tomasz Bogacki. Farrar, Straus and Giroux, 2001. When a new girl comes to school while the circus is in town, she helps two classmates become friends.

Circus Play by Anne Carter. Orca Books, 2002. When Mom's trapeze act steals the show, the least her upstaged son can do is make sure that the child performers stay true to the grand traditions of the Big Top.

The Circus Surprise by Ralph Fletcher. Clarion Books, 2001. When he gets lost at the circus, Nick is helped by a clown on stilts who shows him the whole circus and helps him find his parents.

The Circus Train by Joseph A. Smith. H. N. Abrams, 2001. After moving to a house in the country, Timothy wonders how he will make any friends, but his problem is solved when he finds an imaginative way to rescue a stranded circus train.

Clara Joins the Circus by Michael Pellowski. Parents Magazine Press, 1981. Clara Cow, in search of excitement, tries to join the circus but seems hopelessly unsuitable for almost every job.

Clifford At the Circus by Norman Bridwell. Scholastic, 1985. When Clifford and Emily Elizabeth join the circus, it really is the greatest show on Earth.

Clown Around by Dana Meachen Rau. Compass Point Early Reader, 2001. A clown troupe prepares for and presents a circus act complete with seltzer, a tiny car, and a high wire act.

Clown-Arounds Go On Vacation by Joanna Cole. Parents Magazine Press, 1983. The Clown-Around family has some misadventures on its way to visit Uncle Waldo.

Clowns On Vacation by Nina Laden. Walker & Co., 2002. A family of clowns and their dog pack up the elephant and go on a vacation.

Curious George Rides a Bike by H. A. Rey. Houghton Mifflin, 1973. Curious George gets a new bike and his adventures lead him to a circus.

Emeline at the Circus by Marjorie Priceman. Knopf, 1999. While her teacher Miss Splinter is lecturing her second-grade class about the exotic animals, clowns, and other performers they are watching at the circus, Emeline accidentally becomes part of the show.

Funny Fingers Circus by Karin Blume and Brigitte Pokornik. Abbeville Kids, 1996. Children insert their fingers through holes in each page, becoming an interactive part of each illustration. Add your own fingers to finish the illustrations in this board book about the clowns, animals, and tricks of the circus.

Get Well, Clown-Arounds! by Joanna Cole. Parents Magazine Press, 1982. A wacky family thinks that they have become very sick when they look in the mirror and see green spots.

Ginger Jumps by Lisa Campbell Ernst. Bradbury, 1990. Ginger the dog loves performing in the circus, but she is unable to summon the courage for a new trick until she finds the little girl companion about whom she has been dreaming.

If I Ran the Circus by Dr. Seuss. Random House, 1956. A young boy imagines the fantastic animals and incredible acts he will have for his greatest of all circuses.

Last Night I Dreamed a Circus by Maya Gottfried. Knopf, 2003. A young girl dreams of being part of the circus.

Let's Go to the Circus by Lisl Weil. Holiday House, 1988. Text and pictures present a history of the circus from its origins in ancient Rome.

Little Monkey Says Good night by Ann Whitford Paul. David Bennett Books, 2003. When Little Monkey says good night to the performers in the big top tent, he creates a circus act of his own.

Lyle and Humus by Jane Breskin Zalben. Macmillan Publishing, 1974. Though the circus friends try to mend their broken friendship, it seems Lyle and Humus will never get back together until a swimming accident occurs.

Miss Bindergarten Plans a Circus with Kindergarten by Joseph Slate. Dutton Children's Books, 2002. A circus is planned in this kindergarten classroom. Young children create the show and fun is had by all.

Mister Penny's Circus by Marie Hall Ets. Viking Press, 1961. Mr. Penny cares for a chimpanzee and a bear during the winter. By county fair time in the spring, these two circus animals have taught his barnyard pets many tricks.

Oliver by Syd Hoff. Harper Trophy, 2000. Oliver the elephant looks everywhere for employment after learning that the circus already has enough elephants.

Olivia Saves the Circus by Ian Falconer. Atheneum, 2001. Olivia the pig saves the circus when all performers are out sick with ear infections.

Paddington Bear at the Circus by Michael Bond. HarperCollins, 2000. Paddington Bear and the Brown family go to the circus, where Paddington ends up as part of the trapeze act.

Peter Joins the Circus by Bolette Bonfils. Crocodile Books, 1994. One day Peter sees an elephant at his window. What could it mean? The circus has come to town! There's a seal, a duck, and a monkey, too—but who will ride the bike in the opening act? Peter has a chance to be a circus star at last.

Peter Spier's Circus! by Peter Spier. Doubleday, 1992. A traveling circus arrives, sets up its village of tents, performs for the crowd, and then moves on again.

Randy's Dandy Lions by Bill Peet. Houghton Mifflin, 1964. Five talented lions suffer from stage fright and are unable to perform their circus act. A new lion-tamer is hired.

Sara Joins the Circus by Thera S. Callahan. Children's Press, 2002. Sara wants to join the circus, so she practices and prepares and after many weeks she takes her show on the road.

Say Hola to Spanish at the Circus by Susan Middleton Elya. Lee & Low Books, 2000. See the greatest show on Earth, as well as learn about the event while reading along in Spanish.

Sidewalk Circus by Paul Fleischman and Kevin Hawkes. Candlewick Press, 2004. A young girl watches as the activities across the street from her bus stop become a circus. A wordless picture book.

Song of the Circus by Lois Duncan. Philomel Books, 2002. Gisselda and Bop, true children of the circus, stand up to the snarling tiger on the terrible day that the whole performance goes wrong.

Spot Goes to the Circus by Eric Hill. Putnam, 1986. Spot goes behind the scenes at a circus to find his ball and learns a clever trick. Movable flaps conceal portions of the illustrations.

Ten Little Circus Mice by Bob Beeson. Ideals Publications, 1993. A funny and bright counting sing-song book which features mice who juggle, walk the tightrope, and shoot from cannons.

The Toy Circus by Jan Wahl. Gulliver Books, 1986. From a quiet box in a young child's room erupts a nighttime circus with the dreaming child self-cast as ringmaster.

The Twelve Circus Rings by Seymour Chwast. Harcourt Brace, 1993. Introduces the numbers from one to twelve using the animals, acrobats, and the clowns at the circus.

Where's Pup? by Dayle Ann Dodds. Dial, 2003. A circus clown's search for his partner leads him to the top of an acrobatic pyramid.

Why the Rope Went Tight by Bamber Gascoigne. Lothrop, Lee, and Shepard, 1981. While waiting to see the circus, Mike agrees to hold one end of a rope without first asking what is at the other end.

Word Bird's Circus Surprise by Jane Belk Moncure. Child's World, 2003. Uses very simple vocabulary to describe Word Bird's trip to the circus.

Books for Discussion or Display

At the Circus by Eugene Booth. Raintree Children's Books, 1977. Uses a circus setting to stimulate such activities as counting, noting visual differences, and making up a story.

Circus Stars: The Performers by Kyle Carter. Rourke Press, 1994. Photographs of circus performers and behind the scenes activities.

Name Tag Patterns for Fun Under the Big Top

Name Tag Patterns for Fun Under the Big Top

Name Tag Patterns for Fun Under the Big Top

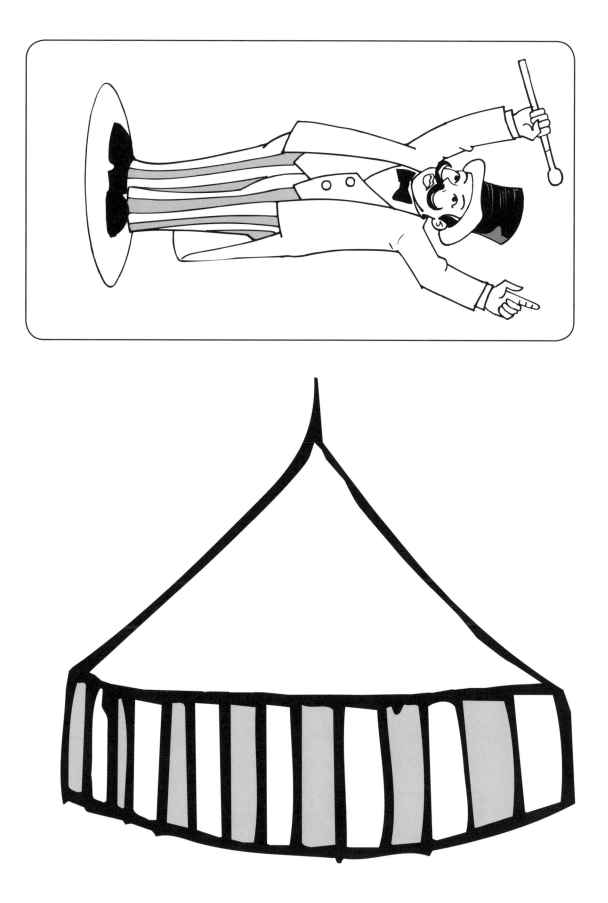

Name Tag Patterns for Fun Under the Big Top

Train Pattern for Animal Circus Train

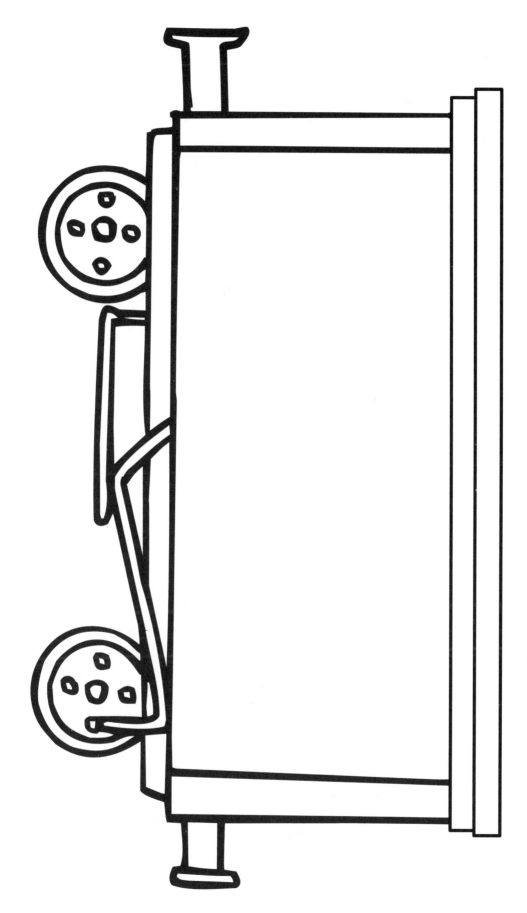

It's a Jungle Out There!
Rain Forest, Jungle Plants & Animals

Before Storytime

Name Tags

Copy the name tags on pages 73–74. Make enough copies so you have one name tag per child; cut out and list each child's name. You may wish to pin each name tag on with a safety pin, copy onto removable adhesive paper, or punch a hole in the top of each name tag and string it with yarn for a necklace.

Props

Wear a jungle "pith" helmet found at Army surplus stores or in catalogs, and have a pair of binoculars hanging around your neck. Khaki pants and a light long sleeve shirt with boots could complete your "safari" outfit. Carry a butterfly net and clip a bug jar to your belt with plastic bugs and lizards that could be found in the jungle. Hold or put in pockets any animal puppets you have that would be native to a jungle.

Storytime

- Introduce the theme by asking the children about their name tags.

- Show props and ask questions such as, "Where could I be going dressed like this?" "What kind of animals and insects would I see in a jungle?"

- Sing the storytime song on page 10.

- Intersperse stories, songs, fingerplays, and activities that fit within your time frame.

Snacks

Ants on a Log

- Use pretzel logs and green colored cream cheese (for moss) or peanut butter (for dirt) with raisins on top for the ants.

Monkey Bars

Spread chunky peanut butter over graham crackers and top with banana slices.

Figs

Figs are grown in the rain forest and many children probably have never tried them.

Discussion Questions

Ask specific questions to reinforce comprehension concepts, re-ignite excitement for the stories shared, enrich children's vocabulary, and influence narrative skills.

For example:

- "Did you know hippopotamuses lived in the jungle?" "Do you remember what Hilda in our story liked to do?" "Why did the other animals want her to stop?" "What did Hilda do that had everyone cheering?"

- "What did the lion king do to stop the crocodile in *Crocodile Beat?*"

- "Do you remember some of the things the animals gave Beatrice in *Beautiful Bananas?*"

- "In our story *Quiet!*, why did papa lion want everyone in the jungle to be quiet?"

Wrapping It Up

Sing the song on page 11.

Songs

The Rain Forest

Sung to the tune: "The Wheels On the Bus"

The trees in the rain forest are so tall,
(Bring arms up high and spread them out like a tree top.)
Are so tall, are so tall,
The trees in the rain forest are so tall,
You cannot see the top!
(Place hands over eyes and look up.)

The sloths in the rain forest move very slowly,
(Climb slowly like a sloth up a tree.)
Move very slowly, move very slowly,
The sloths in the rain forest move very slowly,
So nothing will see or harm them.

The monkeys in the rain forest swing
from the trees, *(Swing arms from side to side and above your head.)*
Swing from the trees, swing from the trees,
The monkeys in the rain forest swing from the trees,
And cry ooooh, ooooh, ooooh!
(Make monkey sounds.)

The tigers in the rain forest prowl for food,
(Crawl on all fours.)
Prowl for food, prowl for food,
The tigers in the rain forest prowl for food,
Listen for their roar ... ROAR! *(Roar!)*

The insects in the rain forest eat the plants,
(Place thumb and first two fingers together; open and shut as if a mouth eating.)
Eat the plants, eat the plants,
The insects in the rain forest eat the plants,
All day long.

The snakes in the rain forest slither and hiss,
(Place hands together sideways and move in a wavy fashion; hiss.)
Slither and hiss, slither and hiss,
The snakes in the rain forest slither and hiss,
In trees and on the ground.

The birds in the rain forest flap their wings,
(Flap arms.)
Flap their wings, flap their wings,
The birds in the rain forest flap their wings,
And land up in the trees.
(Spread arms up high like a tree.)

Put Your Finger On Your Lion

Sung to the tune: "If You're Happy and You Know It"

Use a lion stuffed toy or puppet for a prop.

Put your finger on your lion, on your lion.
Put your finger on your lion, on your lion.
Put your finger on your lion,
Now don't you think of cryin',
Put your finger on your lion, on your lion.

Put your lion on your knee, on your knee.
Put your lion on your knee, on your knee.
Put your lion on your knee,
Tee-hee, tee-hee, tee-hee!
Put your lion on your knee, on your knee.

Put your lion on your lips, on your lips.
Put your lion on your lips, on your lips.
Put your lion on your lips, and blow us all a kiss,
Put your lion on your lips, on your lips.

Put your lion on your head, on your head.
Put your lion on your head, on your head.
Put your lion on your head, and snuggle up in bed,
Put your lion on your head, and go to bed.
Snore! *(Make snore sound.)* Roar! *(Make roar sound.)*

I've Been Walking Through the Jungle

Sung to the tune: "I've Been Working on the Railroad"

I've been walking through the jungle,
All among the trees.
I've been walking through the jungle,
Where I saw giraffes and monkeys.

Tigers, elephants, and lions,
Leopards, hippos, too.
Rhinos, pythons, and hyenas,
Wow, it's like a zoo!

But they're roaming 'round,
But they're roaming 'round,
Roaring, hissing too-oo.
They're all roaming 'round,
You better all get down,
For they are looking at you!

Jungle Hippo

Author Unknown

Sung to the tune: "I'm a Little Teapot"

I'm a jungle hippo, big and gray.
(Point to self.)

In the water is where I stay.
(Spread arms to sides.)
If you're looking for me, don't be surprised,
(Point to self and shake head no.)
When all you see are my two big eyes.
(Point to eyes.)

I Went into the Jungle

Author Unknown

Sung to the tune: "Pop Goes the Weasel"

I went into the jungle today,
I saw a baby lion.
I saw a tall giraffe,
And a poor hyena crying!

Lion Roars

Author Unknown

Sung to the tune: "Did you Ever See a Lassie?"

Did you ever hear a lion,
A lion, a lion?
Did you ever hear a lion,
It roars so load?

It roars and grrrs,
And grrrs, and roars.
Did you ever hear a lion?
Roar really loud?

Jungle

Sung to the tune: "The Muffin Man"

Oh, if I was a great big snake, *(Place arms together and move like a slithering snake.)*
A great big snake, a great big snake,
Oh, if I was a great big snake,
I'd slither 'round the jungle.

Oh, if I was a monkey,
(Swing arms; scratch under arms.)
A monkey, a monkey,
Oh, if I was a monkey,
I'd swing 'round the jungle.

Oh, if I was an elephant, *(Place hands together to form a trunk in front of your body; march.)*
An elephant, an elephant,
Oh, if I was an elephant,
I'd march 'round the jungle.

Oh, if I was a tiger, *(Place hands in front of face as ,if clawing and walk slowly around.)*
A tiger, a tiger,

Oh, if I was a tiger,
I'd prowl all around.

Oh, if I was a lion, *(Walk with pride.)*
A lion, a lion,
Oh, if I was a lion,
I'd be king of the jungle!

I Know a Giraffe

Author Unknown

Sung to the tune: "On Top of Old Smokey"

I know a giraffe,
With a neck that's real high.

She stretches and stretches,
Till it reaches the sky.

She lives on the plains,
With the elephants, too.
You might also see her when you go to a zoo.

In the Jungle

Sung to the tune: "Down by the Station"

Down in the jungle it is really rainy,
Damp and humid, lots of moss, too.
There are monkeys, snakes, and even tigers,
Bugs that fly and crawl, lots of lizards, too.
So many trees and plants, it is really awesome,
Being in the jungle, here with you!

Fingerplays

The Snake

Hissss, hissss, hissss goes the snake through the weeds. *(Make hissing sound.)*
Look, there's even one in the trees! *(Point upward.)*
Slithering, sliding, crawling all about, *(Place arms together, clasp hands, and move from side to side like a snake.)*
Looking for food and sticking his tongue out! *(Stick tongue in and out.)*

Hiss Goes the Snake

Hiss, hiss, hiss, *(Make hissing sound.)*
Said the snake to me. *(Point to self.)*

Hiss, hiss, hiss, *(Make hissing sound.)*
He looks like an "S," can you see?

Hiss, hiss, hiss, *(Make hissing sound.)*
He slithers away. *(Place arms together, clasp

hands, and move from side to side as one like a snake.)

Maybe we'll see him again on another day.

The Alligator

The alligator's jaws are big and wide. *(Form mouth with arms and hands.)*
He has lots of sharp teeth inside. *(Point to teeth.)*
He starts out swimming very slow. *(Move arms and palms together in a wave motion, slowly.)*
But watch him if he starts to go. *(Do above action faster.)*
For an alligator can swim very fast,
And when he's hungry—nothing lasts! *(Rub tummy and put arms out as if to say "no more.")*

Baby Hippo

Author Unknown

One baby hippo, alone and new,
Finds a friend, and then there are two.

Two baby hippos tromp to a tree,
They find another and then there are three.

Three baby hippos tromp along the shore,
They find another and then there are four.

Four baby hippos go for a dive,
Up swims another, and then there are five.

Activities

Edible Art

Forest Floor Cups

Supplies needed:

- crushed chocolate cookie wafers
- gummy worms
- green tinted coconut
- fresh parsley
- 12 oz plastic cups

Directions:

1. Allow the children to spoon the "dirt" (chocolate cookie crumbs) into the cups.

2. Place "worms" in the dirt and top with "moss" (green tinted coconut).

3. Add "ferns" (fresh parsley).

Lion Face Puppets

Read *Deep In the Jungle* by Dan Yaccarino and help the children make lion face puppets. You can also use them with the song "Put Your Finger On Your Lion."

Supplies needed:

- paper plates
- construction paper
- yarn
- markers or crayons
- glue
- unsharpened pencils

Directions:

1. Have eyeholes pre-cut out of each paper plate.

2. Use the construction paper or yarn for the mane. If you choose construction paper, cut it in strips approximately 1" wide by 4" long. The yarn can be cut in varying lengths of 3" to 5".

3. If using yarn, have the children glue it around the edge of the paper plate for the mane. If using construction paper, have them curl the strips around a pencil and glue to the edges of the paper plate.

4. Decorate the rest of the face with markers or crayons.

5. Put on your lion face and roar!

Movable Snakes

Supplies needed:

- rigatoni pasta
- yarn—red and a lighter color such as yellow, white, cream, or tan
- masking tape
- thin cardboard
- markers

Directions:

1. Pre-cut the light colored yarn 12–15 inches long, and the red yarn 2 inches long.

2. Cut a triangle out of cardboard, approximately 3½ inches wide at the base and 2¼ inches high to the top.

3. Give each child one of each of these pieces as well as rigatoni macaroni (approximately 10 per child).

4. Have the children roll the triangle cardboard piece so the base end touches (it will flatten some) and tape the ends together to form the snake's tail.

5. Have the children string the yarn through the tail and tie it at the end. Rotate the knot to the inside of the tail and stuff the end piece inward. You should now have the remaining length facing away from the pointed end of the tail so the children can begin stringing the pasta.

6. Have the children string the pasta on the yarn. Have them leave approximately 2–3 inches at the end so you can assist in tying the yarn around the last piece of pasta. Do so by running the yarn through the pasta and tying off as you did the tail.

7. Tie the red yarn to the end of the lighter yarn (that is run through the body) for a tongue.

Gross Motor Activity

Directions:

1. Each child is given the opportunity to cross the room like the jungle animal of their choice.

2. Have the other children try to guess what animal he or she is pretending to be. A fun way to establish boundaries is to have some children pretend to be trees at the edge of the jungle.

Helpful hints:

- To assist the children in this activity, have a group discussion about what kind of animals live in the jungle.

- Show nonfiction books that have pictures so the children can relate the name of the animal to how they look. A few good ones are:
  Animal Babies in Rain Forests by Jennifer Schofield. Kingfisher, 2004. A wonderful book, not only for the simple text, but also the real photos of mothers and their babies that live in the rain forest.

Atlas of the Rain Forests by Anna Lewington. Raintree Steck-Vaughn, 1997. Shows various animals and life of the peoples of rain forests in South America, North America, Africa, Mainland Asia, Southeast Asia, and Australia.

Jungle Animals: Over 100 Questions & Answers to Things You Want To Know by Anita Ganeri. Parragon Publishing, 2002. Colorful illustrations of many jungle animals with fun and interesting facts.

Tropical Forest Animals by Elaine Landau. Children's Press, 1996. Includes animals such as the jaguar, tapir, orangutan, sloth, and howler monkey.

- As you go through the pictures of each jungle animal, write out the animal name on a large sheet of paper or chalkboard so the children can see the words.

- Write each animal name on individual index cards, so the children can choose a card and pretend to be that animal.

Math & Science Activities

Make It Rain

Courtesy Crystal Wicker (Weather Wiz Kids™)

Supplies needed:

- mayonnaise or canning jar
- plate
- hot water
- ice cubes

Directions:

1. Pour about two inches of very hot water into the glass jar.

2. Cover the jar with the plate and wait a few minutes.

3. Put the ice cubes on the plate.

What happens? The cold plate causes the moisture in the warm air inside the jar to condense and form water droplets. This is the same thing that happens in the atmosphere. Warm, moist air rises and meets colder air high in the atmosphere. The water vapor condenses and forms precipitation that falls to the ground.

Jungle Animal Menagerie

Supplies needed:

- pictures of animals or plastic animals: snakes, frogs, bugs, mice, butterflies, etc. (Include animals that are not found in a jungle, such as cows and horses.)

Directions:

1. Have the children sort the pictures or figures according to categories.

2. Ask them: "Do they fly or crawl?" "Hop or walk?" Have them discuss what they know of each picture or figure they pick up. How many legs does a spider have? Who does not belong? Why would it not be found in a jungle?

3. Count the animals in each category.

4. If you have a plastic snake, use a tape measure to determine its length. Discuss how long some snakes really grow in the jungle, and show the children using the tape measure. Compare lengths of other animals, insects, or reptiles to the children's arm or leg length, and possibly even to their full height.

Fine Motor Skills Activities

Macaw Feather Sort Game

Supplies needed:

- various colors of feathers

- colored paper that matches the colors of the feathers

- Styrofoam meat/vegetable trays

Directions:

1. Place the feathers on a table with enough Styrofoam trays for each color.

2. Mark the trays with a colored piece of paper so the children know which color goes in which tray. You can also write the name of the color on the paper. Using the matching paper as well as writing the words will assist not only with sorting skills, but with letter recognition as well.

3. Have the children sort the colors into the various trays.

4. Once they have them sorted, discuss the letters that begin each color name. Incorporate one of the skills of early literacy development.

Camouflage Game

Supplies needed:

- animal picture or figure used in the Jungle Animal Menagerie activity

- colored paper that matches the predominant color of the picture or figure, along with another color

Directions:

1. Discuss that in the jungle camouflage is very important to an animal. Camouflage helps an animal hide from its enemy.

2. Have the children place the picture or figure on the paper that will help the animal best hide from predators.

3. Place the animal on the opposing color and talk about the difference. Explain that if it is drastic enough the animal might even be seen from very high up or far away, making it more dangerous.

Mosquito String Game

Supplies needed:

- piece of string approximately 57" long

- *String Games from Around the World* by Anne Akers Johnson (Klutz Press, 1995)

Directions:

1. Tie the string together so it becomes one large loop.

2. Read and practice the Mosquito game.

3. Assist the older children in playing the game by placing your hands on top of theirs as you go through the steps listed in the book.

Storytime Books to Share

Albie's Trip to the Jumble Jungle by Robert Skutch. Tricycle Press, 2002. Albie visits the Jumble Jungle and meets such strange animals as a crocosmile, a flyon, and a forkupine. The back of the book also has a Web site for you to take a trip to the Jumble Jungle. Great for phonological awareness (playing with the sounds in words), an important early literacy skill.

The Animal Boogie by Debbie Harter. Barefoot Books, 2000. A monkey, a leopard, an elephant, and several other creatures move in their own particular ways. The rhythm of the text encourages children to boogie-woogie right along. The vivid illustrations, done in watercolor, crayon, and pen and ink, show lush jungle scenes, colorful animals, and a cast of smiling children. A simple musical score is included.

Beautiful Bananas by Elizabeth Laird. Peachtree Publishers, 2003. On her way to her grandfather's house with a bunch of bananas, Beatrice has a series of mishaps with jungle animals, and each substitutes something new for what she is carrying.

The Big Yawn by Keith Faulkner. Millbrook Press, 1999. Increasingly larger animals, from a little bug to a terrible tiger, open their mouths in yawns before closing their eyes to go to sleep.

The Bird, the Monkey, and the Snake in the Jungle by Kate Banks. Farrar, Straus and Giroux, 1999. A bird, a monkey, and a snake lose their home in a tree and go looking for a new home, encountering various jungle animals on the way. Features rebuses, which are identified with labels in the margins of the pages.

Clemens' Kingdom by Chris L. Demarest. Lothrop, Lee, & Shepard Books, 1983. A stone lion, bored with sitting outside the public library day after day, ventures inside to see if it is worth guarding.

Crocodile Beat by Gail Jorgensen. Simon & Schuster, 1989. There's a party going on down by the river! All the animals are there—ducks and elephants, monkeys and birds, even bears and a snake. They're all dancing, singing, and stomping their feet, with King Lion himself leading the song. But they'd better watch out—Old Croc's waking up and he's hungry! Luckily, King Lion is very brave. He'll save his friends without missing a beat!

Deep In the Jungle by Dan Yaccarino. Atheneum, 2000. The lion is king of the jungle ... just ask any of the other animals. All he has to do is open his mouth to remind them. Now a slick lion tamer is promising to make him king of the circus. But this time, the lion might not have such an easy time convincing everyone he's king.

Edward in the Jungle by David McPhail. Little, Brown and Company, 2002. Edward loves to read about Tarzan, Lord of the Jungle, and one afternoon he becomes so absorbed in his book that he finds himself deep in Tarzan's jungle.

The Giraffe Who Cock-a-Doodle-Doo'd by Keith Faulkner. Dial, 2002. One morning all the animals in the jungle wake to find that they have the wrong voices. Rooster roars like a lion, Elephant hisses like a snake, and Snake squawks like a parrot! Giraffe has never had a voice before, and he's certain that he never will. But when he stretches his neck, opens his mouth, and takes a deep breath, something loud and wonderful comes out ... something he'll never forget.

The Great Kapok Tree by Lynne Cherry. Gulliver Green, 1990. Exhausted from his labors, a man chopping down a great kapok tree in the Brazilian rain forest puts down his ax, and, as he sleeps, the animals that live in the tree plead with him not to destroy their world.

The Hiccuping Hippo by Keith Faulkner. Dial, 2004. Many of Hippo's friends try to help him get rid of his hiccups.

Hilda Must Be Dancing by Karma Wilson. Margaret K. McElderry Books, 2004. When Hilda Hippo's dancing disturbs her jungle friends, Hilda tries quieter activities. But nothing else makes her happy until Walter Buffalo suggests swimming and she finds a new way to express herself.

Jazzy in the Jungle by Lucy Cousins. Candlewick Press, 2002. Mama JoJo and Baby Jazzy are playing hide-and-seek deep in the jungle. Lift the leaves and peek through the trees to see where little Jazzy the lemur is hiding.

The Jungle Baseball Game by Tom Paxton. Morrow Junior Books, 1999. The jungle animals enjoy a rousing game of baseball.

Jungle Halloween by Maryann Cocca-Leffler. Albert Whitman, 2000. Rhyming verses tell the story of jungle animals that decorate for Halloween, dress up for the occasion, and participate in the night's festivities.

Jungle Song by Miriam Moss. Frances Lincoln, 2004. Little Tapir is sleeping next to his mother when he is woken by Spider and led deep inside the jungle following the beat of Spider's song. Monkeys, firebirds, snakes, and insects all add their own rhythms to the music, but when the beat stops and Tapir is all alone, he realizes how dangerous the jungle can be. Making things worse is that he can't find Mother Tapir anyplace—where can she be? An endnote by David Bellamy talks about the importance of tropical rain forests.

Junglewalk by Nancy Tafuri. Greenwillow Books, 1988. A wordless picture book where a little boy falls asleep after reading a book about animals in the jungle, then he meets them all in his dreams.

The Lion Who Wanted to Love by Giles Andreae. Little Tiger Press, 1998. A young lion decides he would rather be friends with the other jungle animals than try to eat them.

The Loudest Roar by Thomas Taylor. Arthur A. Levine, 2003. Clovis, a small tiger with a loud roar, disturbs the peace and calm of the jungle until the day that the other animals put their heads and voices together.

Mo's Stinky Sweater by David Bedford. Hyperion, 2003. Mo Monkey loves his sweater so much he will never take it off, not even to wash it. When all the animals in the jungle get together to try to get him to wash it, there's a surprise for all.

One Day in the Jungle by Colin West. Candlewick Press, 1995. Starting with a butterfly, each successive animal sneezes louder until the elephant blows away the jungle.

Peek and Pat Hiding in the Jungle by Emma Davis. Silver Dolphin Books, 2000.

Descriptive words and peek-a-boo flaps make this brightly colored book a fun way for children to explore the jungle.

Pop-Up Jungle by Richard Deverell. Penton Kids, 2001. Ten large bright and colorful pop-up jungle animals are featured with simple text describing the animals shown.

Pop Up Rumble in the Jungle by Giles Andreae. Tiger Tales, 2000. In this adaptation of the best-selling picture book, the rhyming verses bring to life a swinging chimpanzee, a slithering snake, and a crocodile with big jaws.

Quiet! by Paul Bright. Orchard Books, 2003. Chuckling and chortling, sniggering and snickering. The hyena was laughing. Laughing like hyenas do. But nobody knew what was so funny. "Quiet!" said Papa Lion, as loud as he dared, in case his son was still sleeping. Mama and Papa Lion don't want any of the animals in the jungle to wake up Baby Leo while he takes his morning nap. As king of the animals, Papa Lion tells them that he will eat up any creature that makes too much noise. As the day passes, Papa Lion gets hungrier and hungrier, but no one is loud enough to wake up Baby Leo ... until an unexpected noisemaker rumbles onto the scene!

Rory: The Adventures of a Lion Cub by Gill Culliman. Savuti Muti Publishing, 2002. Rory, the littlest cub in the pride, feels that no one in his family takes any notice of him. Everyone listens when his dad roars, so Rory sets off through the bush to practice his roar. However, after trying it out on a friendly giraffe, some scornful zebra, and a troop of mocking monkeys, he finds, to his dismay, that his roar does not have the same effect. But along the way he learns some important lessons, best of all that one day he will be able to roar just like his dad.

Simply Delicious! by Margaret Mahy. Orchard Books, 1999. A resourceful father engages in all kinds of acrobatic moves to keep an assortment of jungle creatures from getting the double-dip-chocolate-chip-and-cherry ice cream cone he is taking home to his son.

The Sleepover by Julie Sykes. Little Tiger Press, 2001. Little Monkey has a sleepover planned, and Little Elephant can't wait! Unfortunately, all the animals can make their beds in the trees except Little Elephant. He's too big to climb trees! How can the friends have a fun sleepover together?

Slowly, Slowly, Slowly, Said the Sloth by Eric Carle. Philomel Books, 2002. Slowly, slowly, slowly ... that's how the sloth lives. He hangs upside-down from the branch of a tree, night and day, in the sun and in the rain, while the other animals of the rain forest rush past him. "Why are you so slow? Why are you so quiet? Why are you so lazy?" the others ask the sloth. And, after a long, long, long time, the sloth finally tells them!

Snappy Little Jungle by Dugald Steer. Millbrook Press, 2001. Bright, colorful pop-ups accentuate the simple rhyming text.

Sniff-Snuff-Snap! by Lynley Dodd. Gareth Stevens, 2000. The rhyming text tells of a bossy old warthog who tries to keep the other animals from using his waterhole.

Through the Heart of the Jungle by Jonathan Emmett. Tiger Tales, 2003. "This is the crocodile with the wide gaping jaws, that snapped at the toad with the big googly eye, that gulped down the spider, that gobbled the fly that buzzed through the heart of the jungle." Rhythmic lyrics and lush artwork are the cornerstones of this jungle-themed progressive story about who started the chain of events that led to the fly—who buzzed through the heart of the jungle—getting gobbled up.

The Very Sleepy Sloth by Andrew Murray. Tiger Tales, 2003. Sloth sleeps a lot. His favorite thing to do is to take a nice, peaceful nap. But the other jungle animals are very busy and very noisy, too. Kangaroo is always jumping on her trampoline; Elephant is always lifting weights. However, Monkey finds out the hard way that he's no good at lifting weights, and Elephant can't jump on the trampoline very well. The animals learn that everyone does something best—and Sloth's best talent is sleeping!

Walking through the Jungle by Julie Lacome. Candlewick Press, 1993. In this traditional English nursery rhyme, a young boy imagines the sounds made by various animals in the jungle.

We're Going on a Lion Hunt by David Axtell. Henry Holt & Company, 2000. Two girls set out bravely in search of a lion, going through long grass, a swamp, and a cave before they find what they're looking for.

Who is the Beast? by Keith Baker. Voyager Books, 1994. A friendly tiger is confused by jungle animals fleeing from a beast, until he discovers he is the beast!

Who's in the Jungle? by Dawn Bentley. Piggy Toes Press, 2001. Using simple clues, the story encourages children to guess what's hidden behind the sliding pages in this interactive 3D board book.

Name Tag Patterns for It's a Jungle Out There!

Name Tag Patterns for It's a Jungle Out There!

On Your Mark, Get Set ... Let the Games Begin!

Sports, Olympics

Before Storytime

Name Tags

Copy the name tags on pages 82–83. Make enough copies so you have one name tag per child; cut out and list each child's name. You may wish to pin each name tag on with a safety pin, copy onto removable adhesive paper, or punch a hole in the top of each name tag and string it with yarn for a necklace.

Props

Wear a sports jersey with a team hat or helmet; carry a soccer ball or football. Try to represent as many types of sports as you can, the wilder the better to get the children's attention, as well as encourage questions and increase their enthusiasm.

Storytime

- Introduce the theme by asking the children about their name tags.

- Show props and ask questions such as, "What am I holding?" "What sport would I play using this equipment?" "What sport do I look like I would play wearing these clothes?"

- Sing the storytime song on page 10.

- Intersperse stories, songs, fingerplays, and activities that fit within your time frame.

Snack

Sports Snack

Supplies needed:

- pretzels, carrots, and celery sticks

- raisins

- peanut butter

Directions:

1. Use pretzels, carrots, or celery sticks to make hockey sticks or golf clubs. Raisins are the pucks or golf balls.

2. Pretzel sticks can represent a pole-vaulter's pole, and celery or carrot sticks can be used to construct a hurdle, with the peanut butter as a base to hold the sticks in place.

3. A yummy way to play with and enjoy a healthy snack!

Discussion Questions

Ask specific questions to reinforce comprehension concepts, re-ignite excitement for the stories shared, enrich children's vocabulary, and influence narrative skills.

For example:

- "What did the man put in the gutters so the boy could bowl in *I Can Bowl!* What is that kind of bowling called?"

- "Jose found something he did best in *The Big Game;* what was it?"

- "Tell me what Froggy kept repeating so he'd remember what to do in *Froggy Plays Soccer.*"

- "Louanne Pig helps her friend Arnie try out for football in *Louanne Pig in Making the Team;* what happened?"

Wrapping It Up

Sing the song on page 11.

Songs

The Olympic Dream

Author Unknown

Sung to the tune: Oscar Mayer song

Oh, I wish that I could be in the Olympics,
I wish that I could run and have some fun.
For if I could run in the Olympics,
I'm sure that I'd be number one!

Substitute other Olympic activities, such as
swim, jump, and throw, instead of "run."

Play Ball

Sung to the tune: "Do Your Ears Hang Low?"

Can you play ball with me?
Can you toss it and see,
If I hit it real far,
Will it fly up to the stars?
Can you throw it to me?
So I can be,
A real ball player!

Take Me Out to the Ballgame

Traditional

Take me out to the ballgame,
Take me out with the crowd.
Buy me some peanuts and Cracker Jacks,
I don't care if I ever get back.

And it's root-toot-toot for the home team,
If they don't win it's a shame.
For it's 1–2–3 strikes you're out,
At the old ballgame!

Reading Cheer

Reading, reading,
That's no chore,
All I want is,
More, more, more!
Yeah, books!

Fingerplays

Here Is a Ball

Author Unknown

Here is a ball; there is a ball.
(Point here and there.)
I keep it on the shelf. *(Point.)*
I can toss it, and catch it. *(Mime actions.)*

I can catch it, and bounce it myself!
(Mime actions.)

Ball? Here's a ball,
(Join together finger and thumb.)
And here's a ball,
(Join together finger and thumb on other hand.)
And a great big ball you see,
(Make circle over head with arms.)
Are you ready? One, two, three.
(Pretend to toss a ball.)

Soccer

Soccer is the game for me. *(Point to self.)*
A black and white ball for kicking, see?
(Either hold up a real soccer ball or pretend to.)
Kick it hard across the ground. *(Kick.)*
It will roll while your feet pound.
(Roll fist over fist; march in place.)
Scoring points is not easy,
(Wave first finger back and forth.)
And you use a lot of energy,
(Wipe hand across forehead.)
But if you get it into the big net,
Then your team will be all set!
(Raise arms in victory over head.)

Three Balls

Author Unknown

A ball, *(Join fingers to make a circle.)*
A bigger ball, *(Same as above, but larger.)*
A great big ball I see!
(Form a bigger ball; shade hands over eyes.)
Now let's count the balls we've made, 1, 2, 3!
(Make each ball as you count.)

Jump With Me

Jumping, jumping, I am jumping, jumping
up and down! *(Jump.)*
Watch me as I jump and as I hit the ground.
(Jump.)
I get higher as I jump, I go so high indeed!
(Jump higher.)
Watch me, I can even jump at very high speed!
(Jump faster.)

Can you jump along with me?
(Beckon with hand.)
Can you jump high too? *(Jump.)*
I like jumping so much, *(Point to self.)*
I think I'll jump to Peru! *(Jump.)*

Do you think you'll join me?
(Point to children; then self.)

Jumping oh so far?
If we keep jumping, *(Jump.)*
We'll become an Olympic star!
(Raise arms in victory over head.)

Activities

Putting on the Green

Supplies needed:

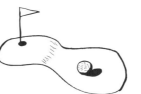

- golf balls
- dish soap
- paint
- green construction paper (1 sheet per child)
- plastic spoons
- Styrofoam meat trays

Directions:

1. Place paint and a drop of dish soap in the meat tray and blend well. (This enables the paint to come out easier from clothing and lessens the chance of staining.)
2. Place the golf balls and plastic spoons in the tray.
3. Each child rolls his or her golf ball in the paint, then uses the spoon (golf club) to "putt" the ball across the paper green.
4. Encourage the children to try to stay on the "green" as they putt.

Gross Motor Activity

Olympics

Supplies needed:

- golf ball
- yardstick, rubber band, and sponge
- large plastic cup
- wadded up scrap paper
- wastepaper baskets
- chairs
- blocks
- small steps *(optional)*
- 2 foam balls
- hula hoop
- 10 empty 2-liter bottles or plastic milk chug bottles
- masking tape
- 2 thread spools
- pipe cleaner
- wooden spoon

Set up:

1. Decide how big of an area you have to work with and how extensive you would like to make your Olympic course. Be sure to allow a fair distance between activities.
2. Mark the floor with a line of masking tape as a starting point.
3. Set up the blocks for jumping or hurdling.
4. Assemble a golf club using the sponge for the putter and the yardstick for the handle, all attached by a rubber band. Set up a cup sideways on the floor.
5. Place a pipe cleaner through the two thread spools, arching it to create a croquet hoop.
6. Place the hula hoop on the floor with a foam ball.
7. Set up the bottles like bowling pins.
8. For basketball, set up the wastebasket a fair distance from a chair or a masking tape line on the floor.
9. Set up the steps at the end, or create a finish line on the floor with tape.

Directions

1. Line up the children, single file, behind the starting line. Have one child begin at a time. Everyone tries each activity only once to keep your line of children flowing smoothly.
2. Start with a standing long jump. With their feet together, children jump forward like a kangaroo in one hop as far as they can go.
3. Next have the children jump or hurdle the blocks.
4. The children then use the golf club to putt the golf ball in the cup.

5. On to croquet! Have the children hit a wadded up piece of paper through the hoop with a wooden spoon (mallet).

6. Next the children go to the hula hoop. You may have them attempt to hula and/or toss the foam ball into the ring on the floor or someone can hold the hoop up so they can toss it through.

7. Proceed to the bowling pins, and have the children roll the ball towards the pins to knock them down.

8. From bowling to basketball! The children may either stand at the line or sit in the chair (depending on how you set it up) and toss a wadded up piece of scrap paper into the wastebasket.

9. End with the children climbing up the steps or simply crossing the finish line, and reaching their arms above their heads in victory. Be encouraging—every child is a winner.

Note: Remember to use descriptive language throughout the activity, both verbs and adverbs, such as roll, gently toss, hurdle, etc., so that even during this large muscle activity the children are exposed to language skills and new vocabulary.

Math & Science Activities

Math

Provide various small balls in a bucket and have the children count and sort them by size and color.

Shuffleboard

Supplies needed:

- 1 large 30-gallon trash bag
- scissors
- tape
- 6 metal jar lids
- kitchen spatula
- marker

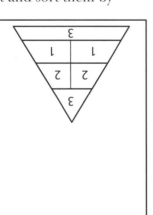

Directions:

1. Cut open the bag, making one large piece of plastic.

2. Tape the bag to the floor at the corners so it is stretched out tight.

3. Use masking tape to divide the board into six sections as shown in the illustration.

4. Use the marker or tape to write the numbers shown inside each box.

5. Have the children take turns using the kitchen spatula to push a metal lid (top up) down towards the numbers. If the lid lands on a number, write it down and have the children say the number it landed on.

6. Repeat.

7. You may wish to add the numbers they have landed on together and show basic math skills.

Science

Provide many types of balls: basketballs, tennis balls, super balls, golf balls, foam balls, soccer balls, softballs, handballs, etc. Allow the children to predict whether the different kinds of balls will bounce high or not, and discuss why they do or don't after they test their theories. For each ball, discuss the size and shape, what it is made from, and what its purpose is.

Fine Motor Skills Activities

Finger Football

Supplies needed:

- Styrofoam meat tray
- 2 straws
- 1 pipe cleaner
- 1 5½" x 8½" piece of paper
- tape

Directions:

1. Affix the pipe cleaner to the top ends of the two straws to create a goal post.

2. Insert the two straws into the meat tray at opposite ends to complete your goal post.

3. Fold the paper in half lengthwise. Fold one corner up towards the straight edge to create a small triangle. Continue to

fold the triangle end up and sideways until you have a triangle shape.

4. Fold the triangle shape in half once again and tape together.

5. Place the tip of the triangle on the table-top and use your thumb and first finger to flick it towards the center of the goal post. Make sure all children are standing behind anyone flicking the football.

Button Golf

Supplies needed:

- buttons large and small (1 each per child)
- deli container lids or clean, empty tuna cans

Directions:

1. Using the larger button, flip the edge of the smaller button into the lid or empty tuna can.

2. Add to the difficulty by numbering the lids or cans and asking the children to flip one button in each numerically.

Tabletop Hockey

Supplies needed:

- baby food jar lids
- unsharpened pencils
- masking tape
- table
- *optional*—2 straws, Play Doh®, tape, scissors, and orange bag netting

Directions:

1. Using the masking tape, tape goal lines at each end of the table, and a circle in the middle for the center circle.

2. If you choose to make goal nets (goal creases), cut each straw in half. Place one straw in each of four Play Doh balls. The Play Doh balls will secure the straws to the table. Place two of the readied Play Doh balls on each end of the table for a goal. Cut a piece of the orange bag netting long enough to fit between the two straws and create the size goal that fits your table area. Attach the netting piece with tape onto each of the straws.

3. Give each player a pencil and a lid.

4. Place the lids in the center circle and establish each player's goal line.

5. The children then sweep the pencil (hockey stick) against the lid (hockey puck) to attempt to slide it across the goal line (or into the goal crease).

Storytime Books to Share

Allie's Basketball Dream by Barbara Barber. Lee & Low, 1996. Determined in her effort to play basketball, a young African American girl gives it one more shot with the support of a special friend.

Arnie and the Skateboard Gang by Nancy Carlson. Viking, 1995. When Arnie is challenged to skateboard down a dangerous hill, he has to decide how far he is willing to go to be "cool."

The Ball Game by David Packard. Cartwheel, 1993. A young player steps up to bat at a crucial point in a baseball game and succeeds in making the play that wins the game.

Berenstain Bears Ready, Get Set, Go! by Stan and Jan Berenstain. Random House, 1988. The Bear family engages in competitive sporting events while demonstrating the comparison of adjectives.

The Big Game by Louise A. Gikow. Children's Press, 2004. A child who has trouble with some of the soccer skills finds an important role as goalie.

The Blue Ribbon Day by Katie Couric. Doubleday, 2004. When Carrie is disappointed not to make the school soccer team, she turns her attention to creating a science fair project.

Bunny Trouble by Hans Wilhelm. Scholastic, 2001. Ralph is one soccer-loving bunny. But when his soccer high jinks almost land him in the farmer's stewpot, he discovers he needs the help of his brave sister—and lots of Easter eggs—to get him safely home again.

Cat at Bat by Susan Schade and Jon Buller. Random House, 2000. Cat manages to help her team win a close baseball game.

Clifford's Sports Day by Norman Bridwell. Scholastic, 1996. Clifford goes to school with

Emily Elizabeth to participate in the outdoor sports day activities.

Curious George Plays Baseball by Margret Rey. Houghton Mifflin, 1986. Curious George's natural inclination to find out more about everything leads him to interfere with a baseball game.

The Dallas Titans Get Ready for Bed by Karla Kuskin. HarperCollins, 1986. Follows a fictitious football team off the field, into the locker room, and to their homes, describing the normal routine after a game and examining the uniforms and pieces of equipment as they are removed.

Dunk Skunk by Michael Rex. Putnam, 2005. Sports actions rhyme with the names of animals that love to play, such as Goal Mole, Dunk Skunk, and Hurdle Turtle. Simple text and bright illustrations add to the appeal of this book.

Dylan's Day Out by Peter Catalanotto. Orchard Books, 1989. Dylan, a Dalmatian, escapes from his home and becomes involved in a soccer game between skunks and penguins.

Freddie Learns to Swim by Nicola Smee. Barron's Educational Series, 1999. Freddie is a very little boy who goes with Mom to the learner's swimming pool. At first he's a little frightened by the water, but soon he's really swimming—and having lots of fun.

Froggy Plays Soccer by Jonathan London. Viking, 1999. Although Froggy is very excited when his Dream Team plays for the city soccer championship, he makes mistakes on the field that almost cost the team the game.

The Great Bunny Race by Kathy Feczko. Troll, 1985. Can slow Toby outrun champion racer, Boomer Bunny, at the Annual Rabbit Race?

The Gym Day Winner by Grace Maccarone. Cartwheel, 1996. During gym at school, Sam always comes in last, but a great basketball shot turns him into the hero of the day.

Hoops with Swoopes by Susan Kuklin with Sheryl Swoopes. Hyperion, 2001. Simple text and colorful photos describe the basics of basketball.

Hooray for Snail! by John Stadler. Crowell, 1984. Slow Snail hits the ball so hard during a baseball game that it flies to the moon and back. Will Snail have time to slide in for a home run?

I Can Bowl! by Linda Johns. Children's Press, 2002. When a boy and his mother go bowling, he demonstrates how to play the game.

Jimmy's Boa and the Bungee Jump Slam Dunk by Trinka Hakes Noble. Dial, 2003. Jimmy's boa constrictor creates havoc in his gym class and his antics lead to the formation of an unusual basketball team.

Jojo's Flying Side Kick by J. Brian Pinkney. Simon & Schuster, 1995. Everyone gives Jojo advice on how to perform in order to earn her yellow belt in tae kwon do class, but in the end she figures it out for herself.

The Jungle Baseball Game by Tom Paxton. Morrow Junior Books, 1999. The jungle animals enjoy a rousing game of baseball.

Little Granny Quarterback by Bill Martin Jr. Caroline House, 2001. Granny envisions what it would be like to be a star quarterback football player as she was when she was young.

Louanne Pig in Making the Team by Nancy Carlson. Carolrhoda Books, 1985. Though she plans to try out for cheerleading, Louanne Pig helps her friend Arnie try out for football, with surprising results.

Luke Goes to Bat by Rachel Isadora. Putnam, 2005. Luke is not very good at baseball, but his grandmother and sports star Jackie Robinson encourage him to keep trying.

Mama Played Baseball by David A. Adler. Harcourt, 2003. Young Amy helps her mother get a job as a player in the All-American Girls Professional Baseball League while Amy's father is serving in the army during World War II.

Morgan Plays Soccer by Anne Rockwell. HarperCollins, 2001. Morgan Brownbear has trouble playing soccer until his coach, Mr. Monkey, finds the perfect position for him.

Mort the Sport by Robert Kraus. Orchard Books, 2000. Mort's attempt to excel at playing both baseball and the violin make him so confused that he decides to take up chess instead.

My Football Book by Gail Gibbons. HarperCollins, 2000. Simple information and basic facts on how the game is played.

NFL 1-2-3. DK Board Book, 1999. NFL stars John Elway, Brett Favre, Barry Sanders, Terrell Davis, and others help children learn to count.

Pig at Play by Susan Schade and Jon Buller. Troll, 1998. At first the too-short, too-slow Pig gets cut from the basketball team. But hard work pays off when Pig wins the game!

Play Ball by Mercer Mayer. McGraw-Hill, 2002. Little Critter tries his hand at a variety of sports, including baseball, basketball, and soccer, while his dog, Blue, does his best to keep up. Includes activities.

Sidney Won't Swim by Hilde Schuurmans. Whispering Coyote, 2001. Sidney says that swimming is dumb to disguise the fact that he is afraid, but with the help of his friends and an understanding instructor, he learns that swimming can be fun.

Slam Dunk by Bob Reese. Arco Publishing Co., 1995. A boy dreams of being a basketball star.

Softball Practice by Grace Maccarone. Scholastic, 2001. Although they are left at the wrong park, two friends manage to have their own softball practice.

Strike Four! by Harriet Ziefert. Puffin, 1988. Debbie seems to be in everyone's way as she searches for just the right place to play ball.

Strong to the Hoop by John Coy. Lee & Low Books, 1999. Ten-year old James tries to hold his own and prove himself on the basketball court when the older boys finally ask him to join them in a game.

Toddlerobics by Zita Newcome. Candlewick Press, 1996. A group of toddlers have fun as they stretch high, bend low, clap their hands, bump bottoms, and generally enjoy exercising.

When I Am Big by Mary Packard. Reader's Digest Children's Books, 1999. A little boy imagines all the fun he will have playing sports when he is older just like his brother.

Willy the Wizard by Anthony Browne. Dragonfly Books, 1995. Willy the chimpanzee loves to play soccer, but he is never picked for a team until a stranger gives him some shoes that he is certain are magic.

Name Tag Patterns for On Your Mark, Get Set ... Let the Games Begin!

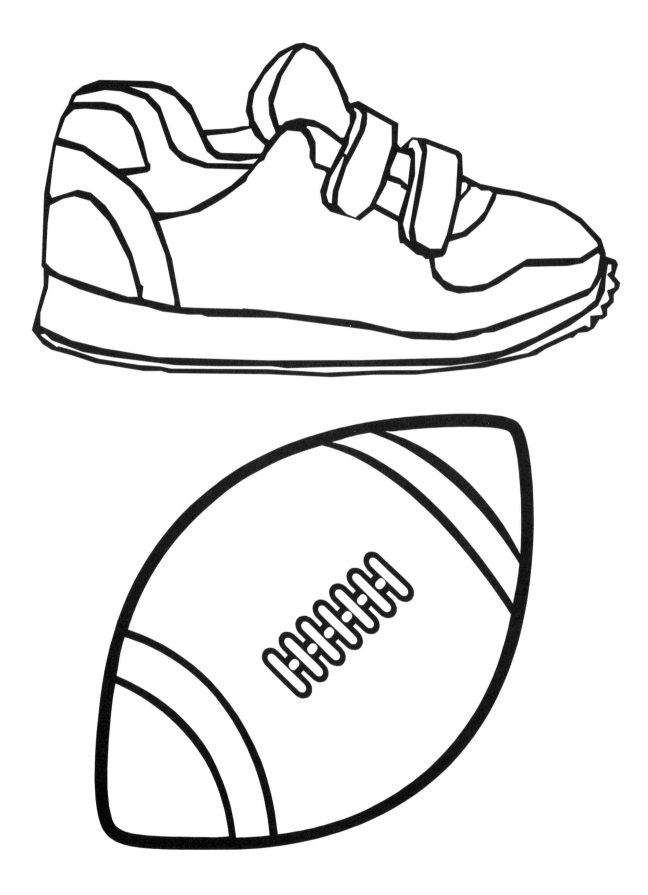

Name Tag Patterns for On Your Mark, Get Set ...
Let the Games Begin!

Out & About
Shopping, Travel, Multicultural Festivals

Before Storytime

Name Tags

Copy the name tags on page 99. Make enough copies so you have one name tag per child; cut out and list each child's name. You may wish to pin each name tag on with a safety pin, copy onto removable adhesive paper, or punch a hole in the top of each name tag and string it with yarn for a necklace.

Props

Shopping

Be over-the-top with multiple shopping bags filled with items, as well as a purse or over-stuffed wallet filled with play money. Get multiple gift boxes and tie string around them, creating a tower of boxes to carry.

Travel

Carry suitcases with clothes sticking out, wear a backpack, and hold tickets (either make your own, or, better yet, use real ones from a previous flight).

Multicultural Festivals

Many people observe and participate in festivals in everyday street clothing. If you choose to wear everyday clothes, carry a nonfiction book such as the Festivals of the World series published by Gareth Stevens. They have very vibrant colors and pictures of native people in festival costumes on the covers.

However, depending on which festival you choose, you may wish to dress as the natives would for the festival. Some traditional garb may be hard to obtain or replicate. See information below for several cultures.

Russia: Warm clothes and furs. Some traditional menswear includes knee-high boots with solid colored pants tucked in the boots and a long-sleeved shirt (no buttons), not tucked in to the pants.

Women wear mostly solid colored blouses over long skirts with scarves on their heads.

China: Wear red for good luck. As part of the parade festivities some people dress in large heads and make themselves look fat to bring prosperity into the New Year. This starts the New Year with hopes that crops will grow well and there will be food for all.

Nigeria: Women wear geles, traditional headpieces in some Nigerian cultures. They are made from cloth and wrapped around the head. During some festivals straw skirts are worn with masks or headdresses.

Men wear loose-necked shirts usually long enough to go halfway down the thighs. On really festive occasions, men wear a wide-armed piece of clothing, usually with a V-neck, and long enough to reach the floor. The arms are so long that they need to be bunched together when worn.

Sweden: Women wear blue dresses with daisies, white blouses, and bright, yellow aprons with daises around their waists.

Men wear knickers with socks, vests, shirts, and hats. Yellow, blue, and red are predominant colors.

Storytime

- Introduce the theme by asking the children about their name tags.

- Show props and ask questions such as, "Where do you think I am going dressed like this?" "Where do I look like I have been?" "Where do I look like I am from?"

- Sing the storytime song on page 10.
- Intersperse stories, songs, fingerplays, and activities that fit within your time frame.

Snacks

Shopping

Serve grapes (great on-the-go-food), and pre-packaged crackers and cheese with a drink box all in their own bag.

Travel

Serve peanuts and apple juice (just like you'd get on an airplane).

Multicultural Snacks

Russia

Fix a variation of Russian Sweet Treats.

Supplies needed:

- ¼ cup butter or margarine
- 4 oz cream cheese, softened
- 1 tsp cinnamon
- ½ cup chopped walnuts (be aware of nut allergies)
- ¼ cup sugar
- 2 tubes of crescent rolls

Directions:

1. Cream the butter and cream cheese in a bowl.
2. Mix the cinnamon, sugar, and walnuts into the creamed mixture.
3. Unroll the dough for the crescent rolls and add a spoonful of the mixture to each roll.
4. Fold each roll over, making a pocket.
5. Bake according to package directions.

China

Serve green tea (decaffeinated), Jasmine tea, black tea, or Oolong tea (these have caffeine), either warm or cold.

A traditional Chinese New Year food is Laba, which means eight precious rice.

Here is a modified recipe (leaving out hard-to-find ingredients).

Supplies needed:

- rice
- dates (red)
- dried apricots
- almonds (be aware of nut allergies)
- walnuts
- raisins
- sunflower seeds (tradition asks for lotus seeds)
- pumpkin seeds (tradition asks for melon seeds)

Traditionally, there needs to be at least eight ingredients, which represent jewels for good luck and wealth.

Directions:

1. Cook the rice so it is sticky. (The stickiness reminds us that friends stick together.)
2. Mix the remaining ingredients and add to the rice.

Nigeria

Serve yams (sweet potatoes) to honor the Festival of the New Yam, a harvest festival celebrated by the Igbo tribe at the beginning of August each year. Cook and serve plain, with butter or a butter/brown sugar mixture.

Sweden

Traditional foods for the Midsummer's Day festival are:

- Boiled new potatoes served with sour cream and chives
- Pickled herring
- Fresh strawberries with whipped cream

Discussion Questions

Ask specific questions to reinforce comprehension concepts, re-ignite excitement for the stories shared, enrich children's vocabulary, and influence narrative skills.

For example:

- "What were some of the animals that were seen in the book, *We All Went on*

Safari?" "Can you remember how to say number 'one' in Swahili?"

- "Name some of the things the girl's aunt brought her in *My Aunt Came Back.*"

- "Tell me a good thing from the story *My Mom Travels A Lot.*"

- "Who were some of the animals in *Around the World: Who's Been Here?*" "Were there any animals mentioned that you never saw before?"

- "Describe a part you liked best in *My First Chinese New Year.*" "Have you ever done or seen any of those things?"

Wrapping It Up

Sing the song on page 11.

Songs

Let's Go Shopping

Sung to the tune: "Are You Sleeping?"

Do as an echo song.

Let's go shopping,
Let's go shopping,
At the store,
At the store.

We'll get clothes and food there,
We'll get clothes and food there,
And lots more!
And lots more!

Repeat with other things children would want to shop for, such as shoes and toys.

Ask the children to tell you what they would like.

Shopping

Sung to the tune: "Mamma's Taking Me to the Zoo Tomorrow"

Mamma's taking me to the mall tomorrow,
Mall tomorrow, mall tomorrow.
Mamma's taking me to the mall tomorrow,
And we're going to get cool things.

We're gonna get new shoes tomorrow,
Shoes tomorrow, shoes tomorrow.
We're gonna get new shoes tomorrow,
While we're shopping.

Ask the children for other things to shop for. End with ...

We're gonna be so tired tomorrow,
Tired tomorrow, tired tomorrow.
We're gonna be so tired tomorrow,
After all that shopping!

Chinese New Year

Sung to the tune: "We are Siamese" (Disney song from Lady and the Tramp)

We will sweep the bad luck from last year.
We wear red to bring luck, for the New Year.
We'll buy things that grow and will blossom.
Tangerines and oranges are awesome!

Mom and Dad give money in red envelopes.
All of us, we'll hold only high hopes.
We know this will bring us even more luck.
We get new clothes and a haircut.
We'll go to a very special parade,
Floats and dragons promenade.

This New Year will be the best yet!
One I know I won't soon forget!

Going On a Trip

Sung to the tune: "The Farmer in the Dell"

We're going on a trip.
We're going on a trip.
Let's see how we travel,
We're going on a trip.

We're driving down the street.
We're driving down the street.
Heigh ho! We're in a car,
We're driving down a street.

We're driving down the road.
We're driving down the road.
Heigh ho! We're in a truck,
We're driving down the road. (Honk! Honk!)

We're riding across a bridge.
We're riding across a bridge.
Heigh ho! We're on a bus,
And riding across a bridge. (Beep! Beep!)

We're riding down the tracks.
We're riding down the tracks.
Heigh ho! We're on a train,
And riding down the tracks. (Whoo-woo!)

We're flying oh so high.
We're flying oh so high.
Heigh ho! We're on a plane,
And flying oh so high. (Whoosh!)

We had an awesome trip.
We had an awesome trip.
Now it's time to go back home.
I think I'll take a ship. *(Make fog horn sound.)*

Fingerplays

I Love to Travel

I love to travel, it's fun you see, *(Spread arms out wide.)*
Will you go somewhere with me? *(Point to children, then self.)*
I can travel anywhere in the world—want to see? *(Place hand over eyes, as if looking out far.)*

People and countries and places galore, *(Spread arms out wide.)*
There's so much to see and to explore.
We don't need a train, a plane, or a map, *(Shake head and pretend to look at a map.)*
Just hop up by me, on my lap. *(Beckon with hand; pat thighs.)*

Come and we'll open up this book, *(Beckon with hand; open hands like a book.)*
And travel around while we look. *(Place hand over eyes.)*
We'll learn, we'll explore, we'll see new things.
As we travel through the pages of what this book brings. *(Spread arms out wide, open hands like a book.)*

Midsummer's Festival

Flowers, flowers everywhere, *(Spread arms out wide.)*
Yellow, blue, and red.
Flowers, flowers everywhere, even in my bed! *(Place hands under head.)*

The girls they dream of their future beau,
Sweet dreams they have, because they know, *(Place first finger by head.)*
They'll soon gather around the Maypole. *(Open arms; move hands as if to beckon all near.)*

We'll celebrate summer with music and song,
Come join in, dance, and sing along! *(Beckon with hand; move feet as if in a dance.)*

The World Over

There are so many people you can see, *(Stretch arms out wide.)*
We're all from different families.
We might be from Russia, Spain, or Peru, *(Point to different areas.)*
But we really are a lot like you. *(Point to different children.)*

We do things the same, like eat and play, *(Mime eating.)*
But we also are different in that way.

You might eat steak, or a burger and fries, *(Point to children.)*
I might eat rice or sweet yam pies. *(Point to self.)*

You might play baseball, or video games, *(Point to children.)*
I play marbles, jacks, and games with strange names. *(Point to self.)*

We're all part of the world you see, *(Stretch arms out wide.)*
It takes you and it takes me, *(Point to children; then self.)*
To make the world over, *(Stretch arms out wide.)*
A better place to be. *(Smile.)*

Poem

Around the World

Author Unknown

Around the world you will see,
Kids sleeping and eating and climbing trees.

Around the world you will see,
Kids running and jumping; laughing with glee.

Around the world you will see,
That kids are just kids, like you and me.

To Market

Traditional

To market, to market,
Jiggidy-jig.
To market, to market,
To buy a fat pig.

Home again, home again,
Jiggity-jog.
To market, to market,
To buy a plum cake.

Home again, home again,
Market is late.

To market, to market,
To buy a plum bun.
Home again, home again,
Market is done.

Activities

Shopping

Personalized Shopping Bags

Read *Molly Goes Shopping* by Eva Eriksson and help the children make their own special shopping bag to reuse again and again. Sing the "Shopping" song on page 86 after or while they make their bags.

Supplies needed:

- brown or white bags with handles
- crayons/markers
- glue
- stickers
- scrap material, lace, ribbon, bric-a-brac

Directions:

1. Spread out the materials.
2. Allow the children to glue, color, and decorate their bags.
3. Encourage them to bring the bag with them when they shop. This will make their shopping time special, but also help save the environment. Suggest that the children use the bag to "shop" for library books also.

Travel

Pack Your Bags

Supplies needed:

- enlarged copy of suitcase name tag on page 99
- crayons/markers
- construction paper
- glue
- scissors
- material scraps
- old magazines

Directions:

1. Cut a "u" shaped opening in the suitcase so it creates the effect of a zippered opening.
2. Glue the edges of the suitcase onto the construction paper, leaving the cut area free to flap open.
3. Have the children draw or glue items into the suitcase that they would want to bring on a trip. They may use the magazine pictures or cloth for clothes. It's okay if things stick out and make it hard to "close" the suitcase—that makes it closer to reality!
4. Encourage narrative skills by asking the children what they would take on a trip, where they would go on a trip if they could, and with whom they would go.
5. Write down their stories to make their "trip" memorable.

Multicultural Festivals

Russian Winter Festival

Read an adaptation of *The Mitten*. Explain that the winter in Russia is very cold. At their festivals they have reindeer races, make ice sculptures, build snow forts, have snowball fights, and jump in the icy water in swimsuits!

Mittens

Supplies needed:

- mitten pattern on page 98 (2 per child)
- crayons/markers
- fake fur
- glue

Directions:

1. Have the children decorate the two mittens with markers and/or crayons.
2. Glue fake fur on the edges.
3. Glue the edges together, leaving an opening for either the children's hands or small animals.

Speaking of mittens ...

Have the children all bring a pair of mittens so they can make:

Ice Sculptures

Supplies needed:

- pair of mittens for every child
- ice cubes for every child
- Styrofoam meat or vegetable trays (1 per child)
- plastic knives

Directions:

1. Ask the children to put on their mittens. Have them think of what they would like to sculpt.

2. Give them an ice cube on a tray and a plastic knife.

3. Have children try to "sculpt" their ice cubes, by carving with the knives. Express that they need to move away from their bodies and fingers in a downward fashion with the knives.

4. Discuss how difficult this would be with a larger, thicker piece of ice. Would a plastic knife work in that situation? Talk about how they must work quickly to avoid the ice from melting. That is why the large ice sculptures we see are always outside in the cold.

Chinese New Year

Read the book *My First Chinese New Year* and then make red envelopes. Discuss the meaning behind this Chinese tradition.

Red Envelopes

Supplies needed:

- red envelopes
- orange paint
- gold stamp pad
- pretend money

Directions:

1. Have the children decorate the envelopes with designs they think would bring good luck. You may wish to have books that will show real Chinese symbols of good luck for the children to see and imitate if possible. Do they remember in the story what was good luck? *(Dragons)*

2. Place the pretend money in the envelope.

3. Discuss the culture and that even the colors are believed to bring good luck into the New Year.

Nigeria

Harvest Festival Headdresses

Supplies needed:

- material scraps
- scissors
- glue
- crayons/markers
- poster board cut to the width of 5½"
- beads, jewels, bric-a-brac, etc.

Directions:

1. Wrap the poster board around each child's head to measure the size. Tape the ends together.

2. Allow the children to choose various decorative materials.

3. As part of the Festival of the New Yam and the Harvest Festival, boys and girls decorate themselves with designs on their bodies. You may wish to use the face paint recipe on page 56 to add a design to the children's faces.

4. You could also use the headdresses for a special parade through your neighborhood, school, or library. Read the story *The Hatseller and the Monkeys* by Baba Wague' Diakite (Scholastic, 1999). This is an African version of the familiar story of a man who sets off to sell his hats, only to have them stolen by a treeful of mischievous monkeys. Another version is *Caps For Sale* by Esphyr Slobodkina.

Sweden

Embroidered Daisies

Supplies needed:

- blue markers
- white poster board
- scissors
- hole punch
- yellow yarn
- tape *(optional)*

Directions:

1. Cut the poster board into 4¼" x 4½" pieces (1 per child).

2. Draw a circle in the center of the cardboard.

3. Hole punch petal shapes around the circle.

4. Give the children a piece of yarn approximately 36" long. The exact length will vary depending on how many holes and petals there are. You may wish to tape the end of the yarn to make it easier to feed through the holes.

5. Have the child feed the yarn through the first hole going from the bottom up. Again, this is a good time to reinforce conceptual language (bottom, top, etc.).

6. Once the child puts the yarn through the first hole, you will need to tie the underside in a knot to keep it from pulling through.

7. Have them continue "embroidering" their daisies.

8. Once they have completed embroidering with the yarn, tie off the end to keep it from slipping through.

9. Have the children color the center circle blue (traditional Swedish color).

Gross Motor Activities

Shopping

Shopping Game

Supplies needed:

- shopping bag with handles
- various items such as plastic food, a pair of socks, anything recognizable to the children

Directions:

1. Have all but one child sit in a circle on the floor.

2. Give the one standing child the shopping bag.

3. Have them skip outside the circle as everyone helps sing to the tune of "A Tiskit, A Tasket."

I'm shopping,
I'm shopping,
My mom/dad (say only one) and I,
Are shopping.

Bought some_____, (Child pulls one item from the bag and names it.)
With my mom/dad,
And on the way I dropped it,
I dropped it.

4. As the last line is sung, the child places the item behind another child's back.

5. That child then gets up and chases the first child to try to give it back.

6. The "chasing" child then becomes the "shopper."

7. Repeat until all children have had a turn.

Travel

Destination Unknown

Directions:

1. Have all of the children sit or stand at one end of the room while you stand at the other as the "travel agent."

2. Each child asks if he or she can take a giant, baby, or regular step to get to a destination he or she names. Encourage them with new vocabulary words for the actions they wish to take and the places they wish to go.

3. The first child who reaches the "travel agent" gets to his or her destination. He or she can either become the travel agent or play just begins anew.

Multicultural

Russia

Tatar Culture Festival Games

Egg Spoon Races/Sheep Races

Supplies needed:

- 2 plastic spoons
- 2 hard boiled or plastic eggs
- stuffed sheep

Directions:

1. Place the children in equal lines.

2. Give the first child in line an egg on a spoon.

3. The object is for the child to get the egg from "point A" to "point B" as quickly as possible without dropping the egg.

4. See which line can go quickest with the fewest drops. If a child does drop the egg, he or she must stop right there, place the egg back on the spoon and continue.

5. Sheep races in Tatar are run with a sheep draped over a person's shoulders. Give the children a stuffed sheep and have them quickly move from "point A" to "point B" with the sheep around their shoulders.

China
Stilt Walking

Supplies needed:

- 2 coffee cans of the same size

- strong string or rope

Directions:

1. Punch holes in the cans and tie the string or rope inside the holes.

2. Allow the children to try walking on the cans while holding the ropes. Be there to support them as they try to walk.

3. You may want to show pictures of real stilts and explain that stilt walkers are in the parades for Chinese New Year.

Nigeria
Canoe Races

Supplies needed:

- 2 office chairs on rollers

Directions:

1. Have the children sit in the chairs and use their feet to propel forward and move their arms as if paddling.

2. Each races to the finish line as quickly as possible.

Tug-O-War

In Igbo culture, people play tug-o-war as part of their Harvest Festival.

Supplies needed:

- clothesline

- piece of cloth

Directions:

1. Tie the piece of cloth in the center of the clothesline.

2. Divide the children up equally and have them sit on the floor with their legs outstretched by the side of the person in front of them.

3. Each child reaches in front of them to grab the rope placing their arms next to the sides of the person in front of them.

4. They pull until the piece of cloth crosses over one part of the center line.

Sweden
Maypole Dancing

Supplies needed:

- silk or plastic flowers and green vines

- hat rack or freestanding pole

Directions:

1. Drape the flowers and vines on the pole or hat rack. If neither of these is available, just place flowers on the floor.

2. Stand in a circle and sing this song to the tune of "Ring Around the Rosie."

   Let's go 'round the Maypole,
   Circle 'round the Maypole,
   Flowers, petals,
   All fall down!

3. All fall together as you end the song.

Math & Science Activities
Shopping

From There to Here—Where Will We Put it All?

Supplies needed:

- 2 oz vinegar

- 1 clean, empty bottle with a narrow neck

- 1 oz water

- 1 tsp baking soda

Directions:

1. Stretch the balloon to make the balloon inflate easier.

2. Place the baking soda and water in the bottle.

3. Add the vinegar and quickly place the balloon over the neck of the bottle.

4. Watch the balloon inflate from the gases of the chemicals mixed.

5. Discuss how we need to take home what we buy. Things like food get eaten and used, but other items have to have a place when we get home. Ask, "Will our houses stretch like the balloon to fit all the stuff?" "Why did the balloon stretch?" "Are our houses made of materials that can bend and flex like a balloon?"

6. Pass around a balloon and let the children stretch it and feel it.

Travel

Parachutes

Supplies needed:

- paper or Styrofoam cup

- piece of cloth, handkerchief, or plastic bag

- 4 pieces of yarn or string (approximately 8" long)

- pennies

Directions:

1. Punch four evenly spaced holes around the top of the paper cup.

2. Tie one end of a piece of string to each hole.

3. Tie each loose end of string to one of the four corners of the cloth (or make four corners from the grocery bag).

4. Tape pennies to the bottom of the cup for balance. This helps make the parachute glide longer.

5. Hold the parachute up and let it go, watching it drift to the ground. Discuss the basics of gravity and how it helps us stay on the ground. Ask, "How is an airplane able to fly?"

Multicultural

Russia

Ice Cube Capture

Supplies needed:

- glass of water

- salt

- 6" of string or thread

- ice cube

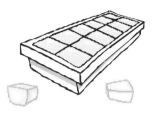

Directions:

1. Float the ice cube in the glass of water.

2. Place the string over the edge of the glass and on top of the ice cube.

3. Sprinkle salt on the ice cube and let it sit for at least five minutes.

4. The salt will melt the ice and then the ice re-forms with the string imbedded in the ice cube.

5. Capture the ice cube from the water and pull it up by the string.

China

Rice Weighing

Supplies needed:

- cooked rice

- uncooked rice

- food scale

- ¼ cup measuring cup

- 2 paper plates

Directions:

1. Ask the children which type of rice they think will weigh more, cooked or uncooked.

2. If you have access to a food scale place ¼ cup of uncooked rice on a paper plate and register what it weighs. If you do not have a food scale, place the rice on the plate and have the children hold it in their hands.

3. Repeat with ¼ cup of cooked rice.

4. Discuss the results.

Nigeria
The Great Yam Challenge

Supplies needed:

- cloth tape measure
- yams of various sizes
- food scale

Directions:

1. Lay all the yams out on the floor.
2. Look at the lengths and sizes of the various yams. Discuss the difference between weight and length.
3. Ask the children to guess how long they think each yam is. Chart the responses.
4. Measure each yam and see how close the guesses were.
5. Ask the children to guess how much each of the yams weighs. Write down the responses.
6. Weigh each yam with a food scale or by holding it in your hands.
7. Determine a winner in the length and weight categories.

Sweden
Blue Ribbon Flower Awards

Supplies needed:

- fresh flowers
- cloth tape measure
- blue construction paper
- scissors
- marker

Directions:

1. Cut the blue construction paper in a ribbon shape.
2. Lay the flowers on a table.
3. Make a chart with columns, such as best scent, longest stem, prettiest colors, largest flower, etc.
4. Measure and chart the sizes, lengths, and diameters of each flower. Use these words as you measure to expand the children's vocabulary.
5. Determine a winner for each category and award the blue ribbon, writing on each ribbon what award was won. Discuss the letters in each award name and ask the children to tell you what the first letter would be based on the sound you make. For example, make a "pah" sound for the flower named "prettiest." This helps with not only letter recognition, but also phonological awareness.

Fine Motor Skills Activities

Shopping
Sort & Shop

Supplies needed:

- paper lunch bags
- small items of various size and color, such as blocks or sorter toys
- markers
- scissors

Directions:

1. Label the bags with the names of the colors and sizes you would like to have the items sorted by.
2. Use the color marker that is the color listed on the bag.
3. Draw a shape on the bag that gives the idea of the size word listed on the bag.
4. Cut the bags to varying heights to assist with small, medium, and large.

Travel
Trip Planning

Supplies needed:

- old maps
- travel brochures—many from various places
- markers

Directions:

1. Lay out the maps and travel brochures on a table.
2. Have the children sort, according to the pictures on the front, for what kind of weather appears there.

3. Allow them to discuss which places look like somewhere they would like to go and why.

4. Open up the maps and explain that some of the words on the map represent towns.

5. Ask the children to look for a town name that begins with the same letter as their name. Have them circle that town with a marker. This is helping them not only with letter recognition, but also with learning that letters are in many places.

Multicultural

Russia

Grain Sort

Items Needed

- dried corn
- oatmeal
- wheat kernels (found at health food stores)
- 3 bowls
- dishpan

Directions:

1. Place the above items in a dishpan.

2. Label the bowls with the words "corn," "oatmeal," and "wheat" so the children can sort the grains into the appropriate dishes.

3. Talk about how Russians have an autumn harvest festival called Sabantui, which means, "feast of the plow." Some people even dress as wheat or corn to help celebrate the crops.

China

Sorting Rice

Supplies needed:

- food coloring
- rice (uncooked)
- bowls
- index cards to label the bowls
- colored markers

Directions:

1. Mix the uncooked, dry rice in a bowl with the food coloring. Mix up several different colors.

2. Spread the rice out on wax paper to dry.

3. Label the index cards with a color word for each color of rice that you made up. Use the matching colored marker.

4. Place all of the rice in one large bowl with the colors mixed together.

5. Have the children sort the rice by color, placing it in the correctly labeled bowl.

Nigeria

Fishing Frenzy

During the Igbo Harvest Festival, locals try to catch as many fish as they can in an allotted time period.

Supplies needed:

- foot-long rulers
- string
- large paper clips
- paper
- scissors
- magnet

Directions:

1. Tie string onto the end of the ruler for a "fishing pole."

2. At the end of the string tie a strong magnet.

3. Cut fish shapes out of paper. If you like, decorate the fish or have the children do so.

4. Place a large paper clip on the nose end of each fish.

5. Lay the fish out on a table. You could place a bubble-shaped piece of blue construction paper down for "water."

6. Have the children "fish" and see how many they can catch.

Sweden

Pick the Flowers

Supplies needed:

- various plastic or silk flowers
- piece of Styrofoam

Directions:

1. Place the flowers randomly in the piece of Styrofoam.

2. Have the children "pick" the flowers and put them back in the Styrofoam in clusters according to color, size, length, or type.

Storytime Books to Share

Books about Shopping

The Awful Aardvarks Shop for School by Reeve Lindbergh. Viking, 2000. Aardvarks invade the Shop-All-Day Mall and turn it upside down with their wild back-to-school shopping spree.

Bear Goes Shopping: A Guessing Game Story by Harriet Ziefert. Sterling Publishing Co., 2005. To market, to market, with a happy little bear. Every day, Bear visits a different store to buy something new. What does he want today? When Bear says where he's going, kids can try to guess. On Monday, it's the bakery. Will he get a bright red apple, a pretty bird, a pair of shoes, or two luscious cherry-topped cupcakes?

Carl Goes Shopping by Alexandra Day. Farrar, Straus and Giroux, 1989. While his mistress shops, Carl, a large dog, and the baby in his care explore the department store and have a wonderful time in this near wordless story.

Don't Forget the Bacon! by Pat Hutchins. Greenwillow Books, 1987. A little boy goes grocery shopping for his mother and tries hard to remember her instructions.

Just Shopping with Mom by Mercer Mayer. Little Golden Book, 1989. Little Critter goes shopping with his mother and his sister and is not always on his best behavior.

Lily and the Present by Cristine Ross. Houghton Mifflin, 1992. Lily searches the stores for the perfect big, bright, and beautiful present for her new baby brother.

Little Tiger Goes Shopping by Vivian French. Candlewick Press, 1994. Little Tiger and Big Tiger meet some other animals on their way to the store, and although the store is closed, everyone is able to get what they need.

Maisy Goes Shopping by Lucy Cousins. Candlewick Press, 2001. Maisy visits Charley to find he has no food, so they go to the grocery store.

Molly Goes Shopping by Eva Eriksson. R & S Books, 2003. Molly is old enough and smart enough to do things on her own, like shopping. When her grandmother sends her to the store for beans, Molly discovers that shopping is not as easy as it seems, and learns a valuable lesson along the way.

Mrs. Pig's Bulk Buy by Mary Rayner. Atheneum, 1981. The piglets are delighted when Mrs. Pig stocks up on ketchup, their favorite food, until they realize it's all they will be eating.

My Going Out Book by Eugenie Fernandes. Ladybird Books, 1986. Simple text tells of a toddler going out with his mom and helping at the supermarket.

On Market Street by Anita Lobel. Greenwillow Books, 1981. A child buys presents from A to Z in the shops along Market Street.

Sheep in a Shop by Nancy Shaw. Houghton Mifflin, 1991. Sheep hunt for a birthday present and make havoc of the shop, only to discover they haven't the money to pay for things.

Shopping by Mandy Stanley. Kingfisher, 2003. A look-and-tell board book with colorful pictures and simple text.

Susie Goes Shopping by Rose Greydanus. Troll, 1980. Susie's mother does not feel well, so she asks Susie to go to the bakery for her. Will she have enough money for all she wants to get?

Tom and Pippo Go Shopping by Helen Oxenbury. Aladdin, 1988. Tom and Pippo go shopping with his Mommy. As Tom samples food, Pippo wants some, too.

Tommy at the Grocery Store by Bill Grossman. Harper & Row, 1989. Tommy is mistaken for items in a grocery store until his mother comes to the rescue.

Uno, Dos, Tres: One, Two, Three by Pat Mora. Clarion Books, 1996. Pictures depict two sisters going from shop to shop buying birthday presents for their mother. Rhyming text presents numbers from one to ten in English and Spanish.

Where Are You? by Francesca Simon. Peachtree Publishers, 1998. When Harry and his grandfather go to the grocery store, Harry races off to follow the wonderful smells and gets lost.

Books about Travel

Around the World: Who's Been Here? by Lindsay Barrett George. Greenwillow Books, 1999. A teacher travels around the world viewing animals in their natural habitats and writes back to her class about her findings.

Bill and Pete Go Down the Nile by Tomie de Paola. Putnam, 1987. Little William Everett Crocodile and his friend Pete take a class trip to a Cairo museum where they encounter a jewel thief.

The Cat Who Walked Across France by Kate Banks. Frances Foster Books, 2004. After his owner dies, a cat wanders across the countryside of France, unable to forget the home he had in the stone house by the edge of the sea.

Have You Seen My Cat? by Eric Carle. Simon & Schuster, 1991. A cat has disappeared and a boy is worried. As he travels around he asks everyone, "Have you seen my cat?" His search leads to many cats but not always to his.

Hot City by Barbara Joosse. Philomel Books, 2004. Mimi and her little brother Joe escape from home and city's summer heat to read and dream about princesses and dinosaurs in the cool, quiet library. This book helps impress that books help you travel anywhere.

Mixed-Up Max by Rasa Gustaitis. Follett, 1968. Two dachshunds trade places because one travels to exotic lands with his master while the other is continually left behind.

My Aunt Came Back by Pat Cummings. HarperCollins, 1998. A young girl's aunt brings her back special gifts from each exotic place she visits around the world.

My Granny Went to Market: A Round-the-World Counting Rhyme by Stella Blackstone. Barefoot Books, 2005. Fly away with Granny as she takes a magic carpet ride around the world, collecting a steadily increasing number of souvenirs from each exotic location.

My Mom Travels a Lot by Caroline Feller Bauer. Fredrick Warne & Co., 1981. A child points out the good and the bad things about a mother's job that takes her from home a lot.

On My Street by Eve Merriam. Harper Festival, 2000. "On my street it's what I see, lots of people and they wave to me." In this simple rhyming book, a little boy points out all the people and places he sees as he and his mother take a walk around their neighborhood.

We All Went on Safari: A Counting Journey through Tanzania by Laurie Krebs. Barefoot Books, 2003. Arusha, Mosi, Tumpe, and their friends embark on an exciting counting adventure through grasslands of Tanzania, discovering all different kinds of animals as they count from one to ten. Included is a section with facts about Tanzania and information about each animal, the Masai people, and the Swahili language.

We're Sailing to Galapagos: A Week in the Pacific by Laurie Krebs. Barefoot Books, 2005. Set sail to Galapagos on a weeklong voyage of discovery! While touring the Galapagos Islands in a red-sailed boat, you'll meet many exotic land and sea animals, including giant tortoises, albatrosses, iguanas, lava crabs, and booby birds.

Where Jamaica Go? by Dale Gottlieb. Orchard Books, 1996. Jamaica has fun and sees many colorful sights as she goes downtown, beachcombing, and rides with her daddy.

Multicultural Books

Beto and the Bone Dance by Gina Freschet. Farrar, Straus and Giroux, 2001. Beto searches all day for something all his own to put on his grandmother's grave for the Day of the Dead.

A Carp for Kimiko by Virginia Kroll. Charlesbridge Publishing, 1993. Although the tradition is to present carp kites only to boys on Children's Day, Kimbo's parents find a way to make the day special for her.

Dancing the Ring Shout! by Kim Siegelson. Hyperion, 2003. The first picture book honoring the long-standing ring shout tradition from West Africa and the American South. It is the first year that Toby is old enough to attend the Ring Shout, a celebration when the hard work of harvest is done, but he cannot find an object that makes a noise which will speak from his heart to God's ears.

Hello World! Greetings in 42 Languages Around the Globe! by Manya Stojic. Cartwheel, 2002. Children from around the world say "hello" in 42 languages, from Amharic to Zulu.

Ice Palace by Deborah Blumenthal. Clarion Books, 2003. A girl and her father help plan the annual winter carnival in Saranac Lake, New York, as the girl's uncle and other prisoners (from the nearby minimum-security correctional facility) work together to build its centerpiece, the ice palace.

My First Chinese New Year by Karen Katz. Henry Holt & Company, 2004. A girl and her family prepare for and celebrate Chinese New Year.

My First Kwanza by Karen Katz. Henry Holt & Company, 2003. A girl describes how she and her family celebrate the seven days of Kwanza.

Naty's Parade by Gina Freschet. Farrar, Straus and Giroux, 2000. Naty is excited to be dancing in the fiesta parade, until she gets lost in the city streets and cannot find the parade again.

Niño's Mask by Jeanette Winter. Dial, 2003. Told that he is too young to wear a mask at the Fiesta, Niño makes his own mask and surprises his family and the whole village. Includes a glossary of Spanish words.

Saturday Market by Patricia Grossman. Lothrop, Lee & Shepard, 1994. Join Ana and Estela as they sell their handmade goods at a Saturday market in Mexico.

Sawdust Carpets by Amelia Lau Carling. Groundwood Books, 2005. Guatemalan and Chinese religious observances, dragon boat races and Easter processions, piñatas, baptisms, and Chinese tamales all weave in and out of this story, which celebrates beauty, religious celebration, and tolerance.

Sweet Potato Pie by Kathleen D. Lindsey. Lee & Low, 2003. During a drought in the early 1900s, a large loving African American family finds a delicious way to earn the money they need to save their family farm.

Pattern for Mitten Activity

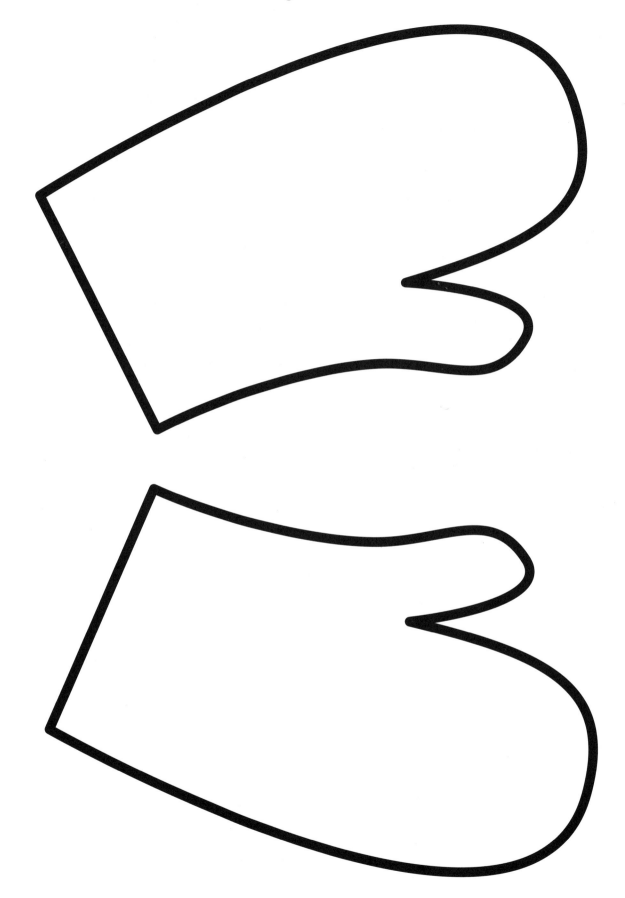

Name Tag Patterns for Out & About

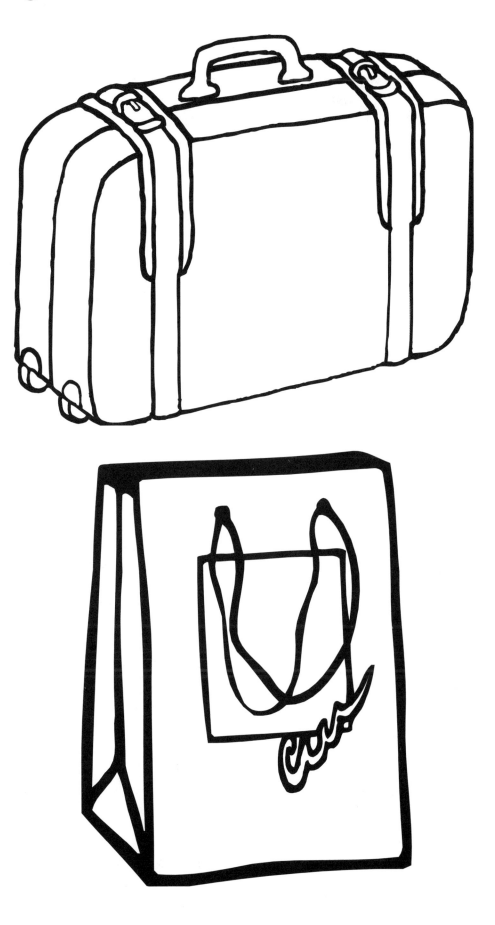

Meow, Woof, Chirp, and Hiss
Quiet & Noisy Pet Stories

Before Storytime

Name Tags

Copy the name tags on pages 111–112. Make enough copies so you have one name tag per child; cut out and list each child's name. You may wish to pin each name tag on with a safety pin, copy onto removable adhesive paper, or punch a hole in the top of each name tag and string it with yarn for a necklace.

Props

- Puppets
- Real pets
- Pictures of pets

Artificial birds and rubber reptiles can be found at craft and dime stores. Place them on your shoulder, on a hat, or in a pocket.

Storytime

- Introduce the theme by asking the children about their name tags.

- Show props and ask questions such as, "What kind of pet is this?" "What color is this pet?"

- It will be natural for all the children to want to tell you about their pets, their neighbor's pets, etc.

To help eliminate the time this can take and so no one feels left out, have many pictures (cut from magazines) of various animals and ask the children to pick one that is like the pet they want to tell you about. You may either clip it to their name tag with a paper clip, or write their name on it, keeping it off to the side until the end of storytime. Call on one child at a time, showing the picture they chose, so they may tell their "story."

- Sing the storytime song on page 10.

- Intersperse stories, songs, fingerplays, and activities that fit within your time frame.

Snack

Serve goldfish crackers with cut sausage sticks, celery, and carrot sticks.

Discussion Questions

Ask specific questions to reinforce comprehension concepts, re-ignite excitement for the stories shared, enrich children's vocabulary, and influence narrative skills.

For example:

- "In the book *Flappy Waggy Wiggly*, which animals could be pets?" "Do you know anyone who has a snake for a pet?" "Why wouldn't you want an alligator for a pet?" "Would a duck make a good pet?" "What color is your pet and what sounds does it make?"

- "Who was the letter for at the end of the book *Larabee*?"

- "In the end, who was the best pet in the book *The Best Pet of All*?"

- "What does the bird do in *But No Elephants* that makes Grandma Tilly happy?"

- "What did the cat want to eat for lunch in the book *Top Cat*?"

- "Why does the little girl bring the kitten home, and why is Ginger unhappy in the book *Ginger*?"

Wrapping It Up

Sing the song on page 11.

Songs

Would You Like to Have a Pet?

Sung to the tune: "Would You Like to Swing On a Star?"

Would you like to have your own pet? *(Point to children.)*
A rabbit, or better yet, *(Place hands above head like rabbit ears.)*
A puppy, kitty, or fish, *(Show a dog/cat puppet and/or do fish lips.)*
Or would you rather have a snake? *(Hiss and make a wiggly snake with two arms together in front of you.)*

Little Kitty

Sung to the tune: "Frère Jacques"

Little kitty, little kitty,
Soft and fat, soft and fat.
Plays with the ball of string,
Meows at everything,
What's with that?
My little cat.

Have You Ever Seen a Puppy?

Sung to the tune: "Have You Ever Seen a Lassie?"

Have you ever seen a puppy, a puppy, a puppy,
Have you ever seen a puppy, grow into a dog?

It grows bigger and bigger,
And bigger, and bigger.
Have you ever seen a puppy, grow into a dog?

Have you ever heard a puppy, a puppy, a puppy,
Have you ever heard a puppy, bark like a dog?

He barks softer, then louder, then louder, then louder!
Have you ever heard a puppy, bark like a dog?

Love Your Pets

Author Unknown

Sung to the tune: "Row, Row, Row Your Boat"

Love, love, love your pets,
Love them everyday.
Give them food and water.
And then let them run and play.

Love, love, love your pets,
Love them day and night.
Let them sleep till they wake up,
In the morning light.

Pet Iguana

Sung to the tune: Oscar Mayer song

Oh, I wish I had a pet iguana,
For that is what I truly need.
For if I had a pet iguana,
My little sis would never bug me!

My Pets

Do as a rap.

I have a little puppy,
He's as happy as can be.
He's softer than my guppy,
And he can play with me.

I have a little kitty,
Who drinks up all my milk.
She is very pretty,
And her fur is soft as silk.

I have a little parrot,
Who likes to eat my carrots.
He shares them with my ferret,
Who gobbles them with merit.

I have a little fishy,
To touch him is so squishy.
So I just let him swim,
Round and round the brim.

I have a little lizard,
His name is Mr. Gizzard.
He likes to hide in socks,
And climbs up on the rocks.

Pretty Kitty

Author Unknown

Sung to the tune: "Frère Jacques"

Pretty kitty, pretty kitty.
Where are you? Where are you?
With your fur so silky.
And your tickly whiskers.
Meow, meow, meow,
Meow, meow, meow.

Peter Parakeet

Author Unknown

Sung to the tune: "Mary Had a Little Lamb"

I have a little parakeet, parakeet, parakeet.
I have a little parakeet,
And Peter is his name.

He hops and flies around the house,
'Round the house, 'round the house.
He hops and flies around the house,
Because he is so tame.

He chirps and chatters all day long,
All day long, all day long.
He chirps and chatters all day long,
For he's friendly, too.

We tried to have him say good night,
Say good night, say good night.
We tried to have him say good night,
But he says, "How do you do?"

Mother Doesn't Want a Dog

Author Unknown

Sung to the tune: "The Battle Hymn of the Republic"

Mother doesn't want a dog,
Mother says they smell,
And never sit when you say sit,
Or even when you yell.

And when you come home late at night,
And there is ice and snow,
You have to go back out because,
The dumb dog has to go.

Mother doesn't want a dog.
Mother says they shed,
And always let the strangers in,
And bark at friends instead.

And do disgraceful things on rugs,
And track mud on the floor,
And flop upon your bed at night,
And snore their doggy snore.

Mother doesn't want a dog,
She's making a mistake,
Because, more than a dog, I think,
She will not want this snake.

How Much Is that Doggie in the Window?

Traditional

How much is that kitty in the window?
The one with the striped, soft fur?
How much is that kitty in the window?
I do hope that kitty's for sale.

Also do variations using kitty, hamster, bunny, salamander, etc.

Where Oh Where Has My Little Dog Gone?

Traditional

Oh, where, oh, where has my little dog gone?
Oh, where, oh, where can she be?
With her fur so soft,
And her tail so long
Oh, where, oh, where can she be?

Also do variations using cat, rabbit, hamster, snake, etc.

I'm a Bunny Rabbit

Author Unknown

Sung to the tune: "I'm a Little Teapot"

I'm a bunny rabbit, *(Place hands above head for ears.)*
Watch me hop. *(Hop.)*
Here are my bunny ears, *(Place hands above head for ears; flop forward and back.)*
See how they flop.

I'm a happy fellow, *(Smile.)*
Here's my nose. *(Point to nose.)*
I'm all furry from my head to my toes! *(Touch head and toes.)*

My Little Cat

Do as a rap.

Pitter, patter,
Pitter, patter,
My little cat.
Rolls up in a ball,
And sleeps on a mat.

Pitter, patter,
Pitter, patter,
My little cat.
Meows for milk,
And it's gone in no time flat!

Fingerplays

Little Friendly Fonz

Author Unknown

I have a little fish, (*Place hand on side with thumb up, fingers outstretched; wiggle like a fish.*)
His name is Friendly Fonz.
I put him in the bathtub,
To teach him how to float.

He drank up all the water, (*Do fish lips.*)
He ate up all the soap. (*Snap fingers together like a mouth grabbing.*)
And now he's sick in bed, (*Rub tummy.*)
With bubbles in his throat! (*Blow bubbles.*)

Five Little Puppies

Five little puppies curled up on my bed.
(*Hold up five fingers and continue by wiggling one finger at a time.*)
The first one sat upon my head!
The second one played with my big toe.
The third one, well, he had to go.
The fourth one burrowed under the blankets deep.
And the fifth one was fast asleep ... zzzz! (*Snore!*)

My Kitten

Author Unknown

My kitten stretches one paw high. (*Stretch one arm up high and continue with appropriate actions.*)
With the other she'll touch the sky.
Then she says "meow" and turns around,
Then gently folds her paws and sits right down.

My Kitty

Author Unknown

I have a little kitty. (*Pretend to hold a kitty.*)
He is as quick as he can be. (*Throw hands upon lap quickly.*)
He jumps up on my lap,
And purrs a song to me.
Now my kitty cat is sleeping, (*Pretend to pet a kitty on your lap.*)
Hear him purr,
Softly, softly, as I stroke his fur.

My Rabbit

Author Unknown

My rabbit has two big ears, (*Hold up index and middle fingers for ears.*)
And a funny little nose. (*Touch thumb to pinky and ring finger for a nose.*)
He likes to nibble carrots, (*Move thumb from ring and pinky fingers.*)
And he hops wherever he goes. (*Move whole hand jerkily.*)

My Pets

Author Unknown

I have five pets, (*Hold up five fingers and wiggle one finger at a time.*)
That I'd like you to meet.
They all live on Sunset Street.

This is my lizard, the smallest of all.
He comes running whenever I call.

This is my birdie, he says,
"Tweet, tweet, tweet."
He's nice to listen to,
And his name is Pete.

Here is my rabbit,
He runs from his pen.
Then I must put him back in again.

This is my kitten,
Her coat is black and white.
She loves to sleep on my pillow at night.

Here is my puppy that has lots of fun.
He chases the others and makes them all run.

Poems

My Silly Puppy

Author Unknown

My silly little puppy,
Came running to my side,
With tongue hanging out,
And tail wagging wide.
"Pant, pant, pant," said the puppy,
"Pant, pant, pant," I said, too.
"Pant, pant, pant" means "I love you!"

"Pant" Said the Dog

Author Unknown

"Pant, pant" said the dog,
As he pleaded with the flea.
"I won't scratch you, if you won't bite me!"

Activities

Black Cats

Supplies needed:

- black felt
- scissors
- yarn
- pipe cleaners *(optional)*
- buttons or wiggle eyes
- metal juice can lid
- construction paper
- glue
- tape

Directions:

1. Cut a piece of felt in a circle slightly larger than the juice can lid (the circle does not need to be exact) and glue onto the lid.

2. Add buttons or wiggle eyes with glue.

3. Cut three small triangles, one for the nose, and two for the ears. Cut an oval shape that is flat on one end for the tongue, (you may want to have this pre-cut—see page 110 for patterns), and affix with glue.

4. Add small pipe cleaner pieces or yarn for the whiskers (yarn adheres much easier with regular glue).

5. Cut a piece of yarn for the tail and tape to the back of the juice lid.

Crazy Pets

Supplies needed:

- name tag pictures (pages 111–112)
- crayons or markers
- yarn
- scissors
- pipe cleaners

- feathers
- sequins
- fishing line
- red construction paper
- fake fur

Directions:

1. Copy and enlarge the name tag patterns onto 8½" x 11" paper.

2. Have the children choose a pet (the number of pets they choose will depend on the time you have allowed) and color.

3. Display the optional "additions" to their pictures—sequins for scales, pipe cleaners and/or fishing line for whiskers, fake fur for fur, red construction paper for tongues (you may wish to roll on a pencil to obtain a curling effect), feathers. Also, have a few extra crazy options such as a pig's tail (coiled pipe cleaner) and yarn tied together for a horse's tail.

4. Allow the children's creativity to flow and practice narration skills by having them tell you about their newly created pet. If time and manpower allows, write down their story on either the paper with their pet or on a separate sheet so they can become proud authors and illustrators.

Pet Treat Dishes

Supplies needed:

- clay plant dishes, one for each child
- paint
- markers
- stickers
- glue (a tacky or quick drying glue works best)
- jewel beads/sequins
- lace or rick-rack, material scraps *
- old newspapers

Directions:

1. Place newspapers on your working area.

2. Give each child a clay dish and have the children decorate them with markers and/or paint, as well as stickers. Remind the children not to place anything on the inside of the dish.

3. Have them glue sequins, jewel beads, or any other decorative materials onto the dish. (Items that have a flat edge work best because they dry faster and do not tend to slide as the glue waits to dry.)

4. Glue on lace, material scraps, or rick-rack (these hold fast and dry well).

5. Wrap the dishes in newspapers to protect them from breaking on the way home.

6. You may wish to ask the children to dictate a story to their parents about what pet they used their new dish with and what treats it holds. Ask that they share their story with you so you can post pictures of the children doing the art project.

   * Because some pets may eat fabric, explain that the children may wish to keep the dish out of the pet's reach. It may be used as a food or water dish if it is decorated with only markers, paint, and/ or stickers.

Gross Motor Activities

Cat & Mouse

Directions:

1. Have the children form a circle by holding hands. One child is the mouse and another is the cat.

2. To begin the game, the mouse stands on the inside of the circle and the cat is on the outside.

3. The children in the circle raise and lower their arms together as the mouse begins to run in and out, weaving through the children's arms.

4. The cat tries to catch the mouse. He may enter the circle, but must make it through the children's arms before they are lowered.

5. Once the cat touches the mouse, they join the circle and two new children are chosen.

Bird, Bird, Cat

Directions:

1. Play a variation of duck, duck, goose using whatever pets you focused on that day. Announce the name of the two pets you are focusing on.

2. Have the children sit in a circle. One child is chosen to begin walking around the outside of the circle and lightly tap the head of each child, repeating the name of the chosen pet.

3. When the child chooses to say the other pet's name, the child who was just tapped must get up and chase the one who tapped him or her. Continue until all children have had a turn.

Doggie, Doggie, Where's Your Bone?

Directions:

1. Have the children sit in a circle and place their hands behind their backs.

2. Choose one child to be the dog. Have the child close his or her eyes and sit in the center of the circle.

3. Give one child in the circle the bone to hide behind his or her back.

4. All of the children in the circle chant, "Doggie, doggie, where's your bone? Somebody took it when you weren't home."

5. The child chosen to be the Doggie gets three chances to point to who he or she thinks is hiding the bone (this is why everyone in the circle needs to keep their hands behind their backs).

6. When a child is pointed to, he or she needs to show his or her hands. If the bone is found, the person who hid it becomes the Doggie. If the bone is not found after three tries, you may choose a new Doggie or allow the child to remain the Doggie until the bone is found.

Math & Science Activity

Animal Detecting

Supplies needed:

- books that show animal tracks such as *Big Tracks, Little Tracks: Following Animal Prints* (Let's-Read-and-Find-Out Science 1) by Millecent E. Salsam or *Tracks, Scats, and Signs* by Leslie Dendy

- cotton balls
- dog fur (combed from your dog or a friend's dog)
- felt
- bird feathers (found outside on the ground)
- fish and gerbil food

Directions:

1. Place the above items out with pictures of various tracks of birds, dogs, and wild animals.

2. Have the children find the item(s) that is not found on animals and pets (for example, felt).

3. Discuss what each item is and what part of the animal it might be from.

4. Talk about the animal tracks and have them guess which ones could be from a pet and which might be from a wild animal. Have the tracks labeled under the pictures so the name of each animal track is written out.

Fine Motor Skills Activity

Dog Bone Sort

Directions:

1. Place various flavors of dog bones (each flavor is a different color) in a large dish or on a tray.

2. Have the children sort according to color.

3. Discuss what flavor each bone is. Ask the children why the flavors are represented by particular colors.

Storytime Books to Share

Aaaarrgghh! Spider! by Lydia Monks. Houghton Mifflin, 2004. A lovely spider just wants to be a family pet—and she thinks she would make a better pet than the typical dog or cat. But every time this clever spider tries to impress her chosen family, she scares them instead, until the day she unwittingly enchants them.

Bark, George by Jules Feiffer. HarperCollins, 1999. When George's mother tells him to bark, the puppy meows, then quacks, oinks,

and finally moos! Like any good mother, the canine marches her son to the vet, who gets right to work.

The Best Pet of All by David LaRochelle. Dutton, 2004. A little boy asks his mother for a pet dog, but she says no. When she agrees to a pet dragon the child decides to rethink her choice of a pet.

The Best Pet Yet by Louise Vitallaro Tidd. Millbrook Press, 1998. A boy and his parents go to the pet store to get him a pet. But it may not be the pet he first thought he would get.

Big Dog and Little Dog Going for a Walk by Dav Pilkey. Red Wagon Books, 1997. Big Dog and Little Dog love going for a walk, but not getting a bath.

Biscuit and the Bunny by Alyssa Satin Capucilli. HarperCollins, 2003. Biscuit finds a new friend in the garden.

Bittle by Patricia MacLachlan and Emily MacLachlan. HarperCollins, 2004. Nigel the cat and Julia the dog think they will have no use for the new baby in their house, but after a while they realize they have come to love her.

But No Elephants by Jerry Smath. Parents Magazine Press, 1979. Grandma Tilly finally agrees to take an unwanted elephant into her home, but soon regrets her decision.

The Cat Barked? by Lydia Monks. Dial, 1999. A cat that imagines life would be better as a dog recognizes, after some thought, the many advantages of being a feline.

Cat Traps by Molly Coxe. Random House, 1996. A hungry cat, wanting a snack, tries to catch different animals without much success.

Cleo the Cat by Caroline Mockford. Barefoot Books, 2000. Cleo is an orange-striped cat, hungry, and all alone in the world, but determined to change her solitary status. So, after a wink and a yawn and a stretch, Cleo sets out to find a home. Lucky cat! She finds one on her first try. But will the residents of the house take to her as well as she does to their bowls of milk and knitting baskets?

Daniel's Pet by Alma Flor Ada. Green Light Readers, 2003. A young boy takes good care of his pet chicken, and when she is grown up she gives him a surprise.

The Day the Dog Dressed Like Dad by Tom Amico and James Proimos. Bloomsbury Publishing, 2004. One day when dad is out of town, the family dog decides to take over his role by demanding some grub, taking the family on a picnic, and hogging the remote.

Dog and Cat by Paul Fehlner. Children's Press, 2003. Due to their obvious frailties, an old dog and a fat cat manage to coexist relatively peacefully.

Dog Gone by Amanda Harvey. Doubleday, 2004. Otis is not happy being left at the Misty Meadow dog hotel, but after running away, he is happy to find his way back.

Dog's Day by Jane Cabrera. Orchard Books, 2000. Dog has an adventurous day slithering with snakes, hopping with rabbits, and playing with toys, but at the end of the day there is something he likes to do best.

A Dog's Tale by Seymour Reit. Bantam Books, 1996. A puppy is adopted by a little girl who is not experienced with pets, so the dog must teach her everything she needs to know to take care of him properly.

The Dog Who Loved the Good Life by Bryan Langdo. Henry Holt & Company, 2001. Mr. Hibble's new dog Jake is very cute and cuddly, but he likes to do human things such as eating at the dinner table and brushing his teeth.

Don't Take Your Snake for a Stroll by Karin Ireland. Harcourt, 2003. Mayhem ensues when a little boy takes unusual pets, like a rhinoceros and a kangaroo, to places usually reserved for people.

Do Your Ears Hang Low? by Caroline Jayne Church. Chicken House, 2002. Two long-eared dogs celebrate their love in the words of a familiar children's song.

A Dozen Dizzy Dogs by William Hooks. Bantam Books, 1990. A dozen dizzy dogs have an adventure with a bone.

Fish Out of Water by Helen Palmer. Random House, 1961. A boy gets a pet fish and does not listen to the pet store man as to how he should feed it, resulting in a big disaster.

Flappy, Waggy, Wiggly by Amanda Leslie. Dutton, 1999. Guess the riddle of who's hiding behind each colorful flap describing the color and sound of animals.

Ginger by Charlotte Voake. Candlewick Press, 1997. When Ginger the cat gets fed up with dealing with her owner's new kitten, it takes drastic measures to make the two of them friends.

The Good Little Bad Little Pig by Margaret Wise Brown. Hyperion, 2002. A boy's wish comes true when he gets a little pet pig that is sometimes good and sometimes bad.

The Great Pet Sale by Mick Inkpen. Orchard Books, 1999. Attracted by a sale at the pet store, a boy tries to decide which animal to buy with his money.

I Like Cats by Patricia Hubbell. North-South Books, 2003. Rhyming text describes how various cats look and what they do.

I Love Guinea Pigs by Dick King-Smith. Candlewick Press, 1994. A nonfiction book (low-level reading) that explores the myths and facts surrounding the guinea pig.

I Took My Frog to the Library by Eric A. Kimmel. Puffin, 1992. A young girl brings her pets to the library—with predictably disastrous results.

I Wanna Iguana by Karen Kaufman Orloff. Putnam, 2004. Alex and his mother write notes back and forth in which Alex tries to persuade her to let him have a baby iguana for a pet.

Just Me and My Puppy by Mercer Mayer. Golden Books, 1985. Little Critter has just brought home a puppy. His parents will let him keep it if he takes care of the puppy himself. Little Critter agrees. He feels he is doing a good job, but the funny illustrations make it clear that the puppy is a lot of work—and a lot of trouble.

Larabee by Kevin Luthardt. Peachtree Publishers, 2004. The mailman's dog, Larabee, helps deliver letters and packages to everyone on the route except himself.

Let's Get a Pet by Rose Greydanus. Troll, 1988. A boy and a girl getting ready to pick out a pet talk about the many different kinds and their advantages before finally making a decision.

Let's Get a Pet by Harriet Ziefert. Puffin, 1996. Discusses all the things involved in choosing a pet.

"Let's Get a Pup!" Said Kate by Bob Graham. Candlewick Press, 2001. When Kate and her parents visit the animal shelter, an adorable puppy charms them, but it is very hard to leave an older dog behind.

Meet Trouble by Susan Hood. Grosset & Dunlap, 2001. Trouble is a kitty that wants to be good, but Trouble gets into trouble.

Meow: A Day in the Life of Cats by Judy Reinen. Megan Tingley, 2001. Photos of cats doing what they do.

My Dog by Heidi Goennel. Orchard Books, 1989. A little girl enumerates the many kinds of dogs she likes, including cocker spaniels, collies, and sheepdogs, but confesses she loves her own best.

My Dog Talks by Gail Herman. Scholastic, 1995. A young boy describes how his new dog Sam talks to him, how they play together, and what pals they are.

My Dog, Your Dog by Joseph Low. Macmillan Publishing, 1978. Kimmy brags to his sister about the exemplary behavior of his dog while pretending her dog with dreadful behavior is not the same animal.

My New Boy by Joan Phillips. Random House, 1986. A little black puppy acquires a boy, teaches him some tricks, and finds him when he is lost.

My New Pet is the Greatest by Sarah Willson. Random House, 1998. Sam's new pet can play catch, roll over, and even fetch. Not bad—for a dinosaur!

My Pet Hamster by Anne Rockwell. HarperCollins, 2002. Read and find out all about hamsters—how they eat, when they sleep, and what one young owner does to keep her pet healthy and happy. Learn about the difference between wild and tame animals in this simple introduction to pets and pet care.

My Pet Turtle by Deborah Reber. Simon & Schuster, 2001. Blue from Blue's Clue's gets a pet turtle and describes what it is like in this rebus book.

My Very Own Octopus by Bernard Most. Voyager, 1991. A boy imagines what fun he would have with a pet octopus.

Nobody's Nosier than a Cat by Susan Campbell Bartoletti. Hyperion, 2003. Rhyming text describes the characteristics of a pet cat.

An Octopus Followed Me Home by Dan Yaccarino. Viking, 1997. When a girl brings home an octopus and wants to keep him as a pet, her daddy reminds her of the crocodile, seals, and other inappropriate animals she has already brought into the house to create chaos.

Our New Puppy by Isabelle Harper and Barry Moser. Blue Sky Press, 1996. Two little girls are thrilled when their grandfather announces that they are getting a new puppy. The family's other pets are not thrilled at first, but come to accept and love the newest member of their family.

Patches Lost and Found by Steven Kroll. Winslow, 2001. Jenny draws, and then writes, a story about losing and finding her pet guinea pig.

Perfect Puppy by Stephanie Calmenson. Clarion Books, 2001. A little puppy wants to be perfect so that his owner will always love him. Even though he makes mistakes, he learns that he is loved anyway.

Pet Animals by Lucy Cousins. Candlewick Press, 2004. Captioned illustrations identify a variety of animals that may be kept as pets. A board book.

Pets ABC by Michael Dahl. Capstone Press, 2005. Introduces pets through photographs and brief text that uses one word relating to pets for each letter of the alphabet.

Pet Show by Ezra Jack Keats. Puffin, 2001. Archie has the perfect pet to enter in the neighborhood pet show: the stray cat that followed him home. It's sure to win him a prize. But now the cat is missing! What will he do if the cat doesn't come back? Archie is a quick-thinking boy with a solution for everything—even a surprise last-minute entry for the pet show!

The Pet Vet by Marcia Leonard. Millbrook Press, 1999. Using photographs, this story shows a child who pretends to be a veterinarian who heals sick pets.

Pet Wash by Dayle Ann Dodds. Candlewick Press, 2001. Wally and Gene will wash any pet—a cat, an eel, a kangaroo, or an ant—but they draw the line at baby brothers.

Pugdog by Andrea U'Ren. Farrar, Straus and Giroux, 2001. When Mike discovers that his rough-and-tumble new puppy is a female, he tries to make her into a dainty dog.

Racer Dogs by Bob Kolar. Dutton Children's Books, 2003. Wild and wacky racer dogs Bingo, Stinky, Wags, Trixie, Dodger, Zigzag, Flick, and Racer Jack all have their eyes on the trophy cup. But adventures await before victory can be claimed—confusing road signs, breakdowns, pit stops—not to mention Racer Jack's penchant for driving the wrong way, which creates a crashing conclusion for all!

Scat Cats! by Joan Holub. Puffin, 2001. Cats cause so much trouble in a house that they are shooed away, and then missed.

Six Dogs, Twenty-Three Cats, Forty-Five Mice, and One Hundred Sixteen Spiders by Mary Chalmers. HarperCollins, 1986. Annie tries unsuccessfully to keep her 190 pets out of the company room to avoid frightening her friend Priscilla.

Smart Dog by Ralph Leemis. Boyds Mills Press, 1993. Set in the country, the tale begins when an old man chastises his dog for lying on the porch instead of chasing a pesky rabbit. "If you were a smart dog, you'd ..." The old man creates ever more grandiose accomplishments for the canine that could make them rich and famous, until he realizes their life is perfect just as it is.

Snappy Little Pets by Derek Matthews. Millbrook Press, 2002. Meet ten different pets, as they pop right out of their colorful pages.

Tiny's Bath by Cari Meister. Puffin, 1999. Tiny is a very large dog. He needs a bath, but the sink is too small. Even the bathtub is too small. The pool is just the right size for Tiny. But it's not easy for a little boy to wash a dog who is bigger than he is!

To Bathe a Boa by C. Imbior Kudrna. Carolrhoda Books, 1986. At bath time a youngster has to struggle to get his obstinate pet boa in the tub.

Top Cat by Lois Ehlert. Harcourt Brace, 1998. Top Cat rules the house until an unexpected box arrives with someone new—and cute—inside. At first, Top Cat doesn't want to share his house and favorite things, but soon he learns that two cats can be lots more fun than one.

Unlovable by Dan Yaccarino. Henry Holt & Company, 2001. Alfred, a pup, is made to feel inferior by a cat, a parrot, and the other neighborhood dogs, until a new dog moves in next door and helps Alfred realize he is fine just the way he is.

Where Are Mary's Pets? by Clive Scruton. Candlewick Press, 1999. Mary wants to play with her pets, but where have they gone? Find out who's hiding in this lift the flap book.

Where's Stretch? by Karen Pandell. Candlewick Press, 2004. It's washing day and Stretch the dachshund needs a bath, but his family can't figure out where he is hiding.

Will You Please Feed Our Cat? by James Stevenson. Greenwillow Books, 1987. When Mary Ann and Louise complain about the troubles they are having taking care of a neighbor's dog, Grandpa remembers the time he and his brother took care of their neighbors' many pets and plants.

Patterns for Black Cat Activity

Cat Ears

Cat Nose

Cat Tongue

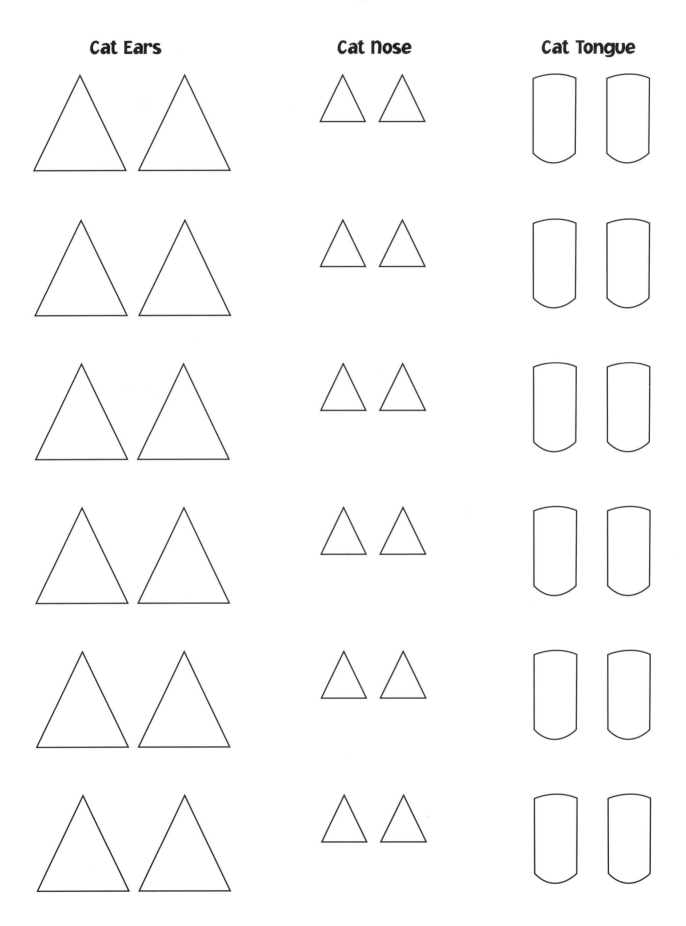

Name Tag Patterns for Meow, Woof, Chirp, and Hiss

Our Sensational Senses
Body Awareness, Five Senses

Before Storytime

Name Tags

Copy the name tags on page 122. Make enough copies so you have one name tag per child; cut out and list each child's name. You may wish to pin each name tag on with a safety pin, copy onto removable adhesive paper, or punch a hole in the top of each name tag and string it with yarn for a neck-lace.

Props

- coffee beans in a jar (smell)
- an animal skin, fake fur, or cotton balls in a bag (touch/feel)
- small cookies, fruit, or a piece of candy—one per child (taste)
- a bell or timer (hearing)
- a pair of big glasses and/or a magnifying glass (sight)

Note: Due to allergies it is best to have your "taste" item packaged to go so the children may eat it at home.

Storytime

- For this theme, you may wish to incorporate some simple sign language words into your stories. Choose simple words like "run," "touch," "see," etc., and look in simple sign language books or on the Internet at **www.masterstech-home.com/ASLDict.html** for a basic dictionary of American Sign Language.

- Use the program as a catalyst to discuss people with disabilities. Explain that they have five senses too, but they might not work the same as ours. You may also wish to bring in books in Braille (available at many larger libraries).

- Introduce the theme by discussing the name tags. Ask the children to think about what the name tag might mean to this storytime.

- Sing the storytime song on page 10.

- Intersperse stories, fingerplays, songs, and activities to fit your theme and time frame.

Snack

- Finger Jell-O (see it wiggle, touch it, and feel the cold)

- Orange slices (smell it and taste it)

- Celery sticks (hear the crunch)

- Have the children note the various colors (sight), sounds (hearing), textures (touch), smells, and tastes.

Discussion Questions

Ask specific questions to reinforce comprehension concepts, re-ignite excitement for the stories shared, enrich children's vocabulary, and influence narrative skills.

For example:

- "What does warthog do that causes all the things to happen in *Slop Goes the Soup?*"

- "In the book *First Delights,* what does Sally hold in spring?"

- "What was rabbit's story in *Forest Friends Five Senses?*" "What sense was not working well and who helped him?"

- "Which four senses are used when you play with a puppy as shown in *My Five Senses?*"

- "Who stung (touched) the girl in *I Saw the Sea and the Sea Saw Me*?"

Wrapping It Up

Sing the song on page 11.

Songs

Our Bodies

Sung to the tune: "The Wheels On the Bus"

The arms on our bodies go up and down,
Up and down, up and down,
The arms on our bodies go up and down,
And help us hug!

The toes on our feet they wiggle and scrunch,
Wiggle and scrunch, wiggle and scrunch,
The toes on our feet they wiggle and scrunch,
And help us walk!

The legs on our bodies move back and forth,
Back and forth, back and forth,
The legs on our bodies move back and forth,
And help us stand!

The knees on our bodies they
bend and stretch,
Bend and stretch, bend and stretch,
The knees on our bodies they
bend and stretch,
And help us move!

The waists on our bodies they twist and turn,
Twist and turn, twist and turn,
The waists on our bodies they twist and turn,
And help us bend!

The hands on our bodies they
bend and shake,
Bend and shake, bend and shake,
The hands on our bodies they
bend and shake,
And wave goodbye!

Rat-a-Tat-Tat

Do as a rap.

Rat-a-tat tat, we climb the stairs like that.
Thump-a-bump-bump,
We open the door like that.
Splat-a-splat-splat,
We wash our hands like that.
Pat-a-pat-pat, we make the bread like that.
Smoosh-a-goosh-goosh,
We spread the jam like that.

Splish–a-splish-splash,
We pour the milk like that.
Yum-a-dum-dum, we eat our lunch like that.
Sleepy-ho-hum, we take a nap like that ...
SNORE! ZZZZZZZZZZZZZ

Ears, Eyes, Tongue, and Nose

Sung to the tune: "Head, Shoulders, Knees, and Toes"

Ears, eyes, tongue, and nose, *(Point to the various body parts.)*
Tongue and nose.
Ears, eyes, tongue, and nose,
And fingers that feel and touch your toes.
Ears, eyes, tongue, and nose,
Tongue and nose.

Repeat the song and only mouth the words, do not make a sound.

Note: Explain that this is a bit like what a deaf person would experience, so sometimes they read lips, trying to decipher what a person is saying by the movement of their mouth.

Show how it is difficult to read lips when we bend our heads down to touch our toes or show our tongues.

Wiggly Body Parts

Sung to the tune: "The Farmer in the Dell"

Let's wiggle our fingers, they're part of our hands,
They help us touch and feel,
Let's wiggle our fingers.

Let's wiggle our nose, it's part of our face,
It smells everything,
Let's wiggle our nose.

Let's wag our tongue, out of our mouth,
We taste salty, sour, or sweet,
With our tongue.

Let's flap our ears, on the side of our face,
What do you hear, as you flap them on your head?

Let's blink our eyes, on the center of our face,
They help us see things all over the place.

Let's wiggle all of me,
Let's wiggle all of me.
I feel, hear, and see,
When I wiggle all of me!

Fingerplay

Our Five Senses

My ears are to hear, *(Touch ears.)*
My eyes are to see, *(Point to eyes.)*
They also tear, when I'm sad or happy.

My nose is to smell, *(Point to nose.)*
My tongue tastes my food,
(Point to mouth; stick tongue out.)
And helps me to talk and tell you my mood.

My fingers they touch, they feel, and they
hold, *(Hold up hand, wiggle fingers.)*
They help me to know what is hot
and what's cold.

So now you know the five senses of me,
(Show five fingers, point to self.)
You have them, too, as you can see.
(Point to children.)
Use them daily to hear, taste, touch,
smell, and see,
And you will be happy as can be! *(Smile.)*

Two Little Eyes

Author Unknown

Two little eyes to look around.
Two little ears to hear each sound.
One little nose that smells what's sweet.
One little mouth that likes to eat.

I Have

Author Unknown

I have ten fingers, I have ten toes.
(Point to appropriate body parts.)
I have two ears, and one little nose.
I have two eyes, one mouth, one chin.
I have one tongue that moves out and in.
(Stick tongue in and out.)

I Have Five Senses

I have five senses just like you.
(Hold up five fingers.)
I'll name them all, can you, too?
(Point to children.)
There's hearing, sight, taste, and smell.
(Point to ears, eyes, mouth and nose.)
And one I missed, can you tell?
(Hold up one finger; point to children.)
Something you'd get after you fell.
A hug would use our sense of touch,

(Hug self; show hand.)
One thing I like very much! *(Point to self.)*

Look What I Can Do!

My ears hear the sound of rat-a-tat-tat.
(Point to ears; stomp feet.)
My hands they go pat-a-pat-pat.
(Show hands; pat thighs.)
My tongue it can taste all the good things to eat.
(Point to mouth.)
My nose smells scents, nasty, and sweet.
(Point to nose; hold nose then inhale deeply.)
My eyes see yours as they meet. *(Point to eyes.)*
Looking at your smiling faces is such a treat!
(Smile.)

Five Senses

Author Unknown

Smelling is just so divine, *(Sniff air.)*
I do it with my nose so fine. *(Point to nose.)*

Hearing is a great delight, *(Cup ears.)*
I use my ears left and right.
(Point to left, then right, ear.)

Tasting is a special treat, *(Point to mouth.)*
I love my tongue on something sweet.
(Lick lips.)

Seeing brings the world in view,
(Focus a telescope.)
See my eyes here, one and two. *(Point to eyes.)*

Touching is fun and oh so easy, *(Wiggle fingers.)*
'Cause I can feel with all of me.
(Wiggle whole body.)

My Senses Work For Me

I hear with my ears, *(Touch ears.)*
My eyes they cry tears, *(Point to eyes.)*
And help see the world around me.
(Spread arms out wide.)

My mouth has a tongue that tastes sour or sweet,
(Point to mouth, stick out tongue.)
My touch tells when I'm near cold or heat.
(Show hands.)

My nose it smells the good and the bad.
(Point to nose.)
Whether I'm happy or whether I'm sad.
(Smile; look sad.)
All five senses work for me, *(Show five fingers.)*
So I can touch, smell, hear, taste, and see!
(Wiggle fingers, touch nose, ears, mouth, and eyes.)

Activities

My Five Senses Face

Supplies needed:

- paper plates (1 per child)
- old magazines or pictures
- glue
- scissors
- yarn
- crayons or markers
- red construction paper
- eyes, ears, nose, hand, and mouth from pages 123–124
- unsharpened pencil (*optional*)

Directions:

1. Look for pictures of things that can be seen, heard, tasted, smelled, or touched. Have them pre-cut or give the children old magazines so they can cut them out. Use this as a time for "what" questions (dialogic skills). Ask the children, "What would this taste like?" or "What sound does that make?"

2. Glue each corresponding picture to the paper plate where the eyes, nose, and ears would go.

3. Cut a tongue from the red construction paper and glue the picture of what you would taste to the tip of the tongue.

4. Cut out the eyes, ears, nose, hand, and mouth for each child.

5. Apply a bit of glue to the edge of the eyes, ears, nose, and mouth and place on the plate over the pictures to create a lift-the–flap effect.

6. Attach the tongue under the mouth. To create a hidden effect on the tongue, roll the tongue with an unsharpened pencil so it curls up under the mouth.

7. Glue the hand to the back of the paper plate and attach the "touch" picture to the hand.

8. Color the face and glue on yarn for hair.

Tasty Painting

Supplies needed:

- instant chocolate pudding
- 1½ tsp mint extract
- paper
- plastic spoons (1 per child)
- individual cups (1 per child)

Directions:

1. Mix up the pudding according to directions.

2. Add mint extract.

3. Spoon pudding into individual cups.

4. Give each child a cup of pudding and a spoon.

5. Ask the children to use their hearing first by listening to claps.

   - Clap once—they taste the pudding with the spoon.
   - Clap twice—they smell the pudding with their nose.
   - Clap three times—they touch the pudding with their hands and paint on the paper.

6. See what pictures they can make.

Gross Motor Activity

Touch Relay

Supplies needed:

- 2 paper bags
- rough and smooth items (equal number of items needed for each bag; 1 item per child)
- 4 baskets
- signs for baskets

Directions:

1. Prepare the bags by placing the same number of items in each bag. The rough and smooth items do not have to be equal.

2. Label the baskets with the words "rough" and "smooth" and place a sample item on each label.

3. Have the children form two lines.

4. Place the baskets at the opposite end of where you will start, with one of each basket (rough and smooth) in line with the two lines of children.

5. The first child from each line chooses one item from the bag and then quickly moves to the other end to deposit the item in the appropriate basket.

6. Continue with all of the children.

7. You may wish to tally the number of each kind of item for both teams.

Sniff-a-Scent

Supplies needed:

- cinnamon

- coffee beans

- lemon juice

- 3 containers (preferably not clear)

Directions:

1. Place the cinnamon in one container, the coffee beans in another container, and the lemon juice in the last container.

2. Line the children up and have them choose one container to sniff.

3. Ask that they skip or hop across the room if they like the smell, and crawl if they do not.

4. You can do this as many times as you have items to smell, and you may even wish to chart how many children liked or did not like each scent.

Listening Ears

Item Needed:

- bell

Directions:

1. Ask the children to turn up their "listening ears" for this activity.

2. When the children hear a bell ring, have them move in whatever way makes them happy, so long as they do not bump into anything or anyone.

3. When the bell rings two times, they stop.

Watch and See

Supplies needed:

- red and green construction paper

Directions:

Hold up a piece of green construction paper. Explain that when they see this color paper they can run or march in place. When you show a piece of red construction paper, they stop. Let them know they need to be watching with their eyes to play this game.

A good way to segue into the snack is to say, "Which of the five senses did we not just play a game for?" "Taste!" "So now let's have snack!"

Math & Science Activities

What's that Smell?

Supplies needed:

- 2 glasses

- white vinegar

- water

Directions:

1. Fill one glass with water and the other with vinegar.

2. Have the children smell the two glasses and try to identify the odor and what it might be.

What Do I Hear?

Supplies needed:

- medium-sized gift boxes

- tape

- rocks

- cotton balls

- other items of varying weight and sounds

Directions:

1. Place the different items in the boxes (one type of item in each).

2. Have the children try to guess what could be in the boxes by the sound.

"See" Sound Science Experiment

Supplies needed:

- plastic wrap
- glass
- rubber band
- salt
- wooden spoon and metal lid or drum

Directions:

1. Place plastic wrap over a glass and tightly affix using a rubber band.

2. Place salt on top of the plastic wrap.

3. Have the children beat a drum, or tap a lid with a wooden spoon near the glass to produce loud sounds.

4. Watch how the plastic wrap vibrates the salt, allowing the children to see how sound vibrates through the air.

Does Color Have a Taste?

Add food coloring to water. Show the children the various colored waters. Have someone close his or her eyes and see if he or she can "taste" which color it is.

Touch Center

Supplies needed:

- blindfold
- box
- feather
- cotton ball
- piece of cloth
- bubble wrap
- soft side of Velcro

Directions:

1. Show each item and say its name.

2. Place the items in the box.

3. Blindfold a willing child and have him or her guess what item he or she is touching.

4. Have the child show the item after his or her guess.

Fine Motor Skills Activities

Five Senses Awareness*

* You may wish to use this activity to discuss impairments some people have. Help the children understand that even when we have differences we are all equal.

Set up five areas of exploration.

Tasting area:

- Place sugar in one dish and salt in another. With a small spoon, give the children a taste of each, one at a time. Do they know what each taste is? Discuss how they both look the same (so their eyes are not a help here) but taste different.

- What part of their body helps them tell the difference? Place two different flavored jelly beans out on the table. Ask, "They are different colors, so we know they will taste different, right?" Have them close their eyes and pinch their noses. Give them one jelly bean at a time. They will not be able to tell one from the other. This is because we need our sense of smell to taste. Just like when we have a cold, we cannot taste as well.

- Allow other tastes to be experienced, such as maple syrup and molasses, sweetened lemonade and lemon juice. They all may look alike, but how are they different? Do they notice some people like tastes others do not? Many of us have the same senses but we are not all alike.

Scent area:

- Fill baby food jars with various scents, such as: coffee beans, a cotton ball sprayed with perfume, baby powder, cinnamon, lemon juice. Have the children say which scent they like best and if it reminds them of anything.

Sound area:

- Fill glasses with varying levels of water in each and tap gently with a spoon. Ask the children to hear the different high and low sounds. If you place a straw in the water, and move the straw up and down, it will change the pitch.

- Have various items out for the children to interact with and discover the various sounds they can make, such as small water bottles filled about one third full with dried beans, peas or rice, bells, plastic spoons, plastic food containers with lids, oatmeal boxes with lids, a shoe box without a lid, and rubber bands stretched across.

Sight area:

- Blindfold any willing child and ask him or her what he or she sees. How can you safely move around without sight? How would you read a book, or see colors?

- Those who are not comfortable wearing a blindfold can place their hands over their eyes.

- Play a game with various colored milk caps, balls, or any items of different colors that look and feel similar. Ask the blindfolded child to pick up a specific color.

Touch area:

- Inside a bag place various tactile objects, such as an ice pack (like the kind found in First Aid kits), a piece of sandpaper, a soft or furry cloth, a smooth rock. Ask the children to say how it feels before they remove it from the bag. Encourage them to use descriptive language.

In addition to the above areas, play "what is it" for each of the five senses:

"What does it taste like?"

"What does it smell like?"

"What does it sound like (high or low)?"

"What do you do when you cannot see?"

"What dangers would we have if we could not feel?"

Storytime Books to Share

All the Way to Morning by Marc Harshman. Marshall Cavendish, 1999. All around the world, different children hear different sounds as they get ready to sleep.

The Baby Goes Beep by Rebecca O'Connell. Roaring Brook Press, 2003. A baby makes various sounds as he explores the world around him.

Busy, Busy City Street by Cari Meister. Viking, 2000. A simple rhyming story featuring sounds you might hear in the city.

City Sounds by Craig Brown. Greenwillow Books, 1992. Enumerates the many different sounds a visitor might hear in the city, including the honking of trucks, the sound of a jackhammer, and the bonging of a big clock.

Disney's Winnie the Pooh Senses by Rachel Smith. Mouse Works, 2000. A simple story that explains the five senses and how they can help a hungry Pooh Bear find a sweet treat.

The Ear Book by Al Perkins. Random House, 1968. A boy and his dog listen to the world around them.

Eyes, Nose, Fingers, and Toes: A First Book About You by Judy Hindley. Candlewick Press, 1999. A group of toddlers demonstrate all the fun things that they can do with their eyes, ears, mouths, hands, legs, feet—and everything in between.

First Delights: A Book About the Five Senses by Tasha Tudor. Platt & Munk Publishers, 1988. Go through Sally's year on the farm and how she uses her five senses throughout the seasons.

Forest Friends Five Senses by Cristina Garelli. Knopf, 2001. Animal friends share their experiences with the five senses.

A Head is for Hats by Mary Serfozo. Scholastic, 1999. The charming text in this rhyming book follows a boy and girl as they play dress-up. Different body parts—eyes, nose, mouth, hands, feet—are pointed out with each fun change of costume they make. An amusing way to teach young children about body parts.

Hearing by María Rius. Barron's, 1985. Text and illustrations present an array of sounds. Included is a short scientific explanation of our sense of hearing, with a diagram of the ear.

Hear That? by Tama Janowitz and Tracy Dockray. Seastar Books, 2001. Colorful pictures and a text chock-full of sounds tell a story of a mother and child as they wonder what each click, knock, and rattle in their house could possibly be. With each guess their thoughts get wilder and wilder.

Hello Ocean! by Pam Muñoz Ryan. Talewinds, 2001. Using rhyming text, a child describes the wonder of the ocean experience through each of her five senses.

I Saw the Sea and the Sea Saw Me by Megan Montague Cash. Viking, 2001. A girl enjoys using all of her five senses to explore the ocean, but when a jellyfish appears she discovers that the sea is not always nice.

It Looked Like Spilt Milk by Charles Shaw. HarperCollins, 1947. Our eyes can be deceiving. White shapes silhouetted against a blue background change on every page. Is it a rabbit, a bird, or just spilt milk?

Jazz Baby by Carole Boston Weatherford. Lee & Low, 2002. A group of toddlers move and play, hum and sleep to a jazz beat.

Let's Get the Rhythm by Anne Miranda. Scholastic, 1994. Feel the rhythm that your body makes in this interactive book told in chant.

My Five Senses by Aliki. Thomas Crowell, 1989. A simple presentation of the five senses, demonstrating some ways we use them.

The Nose Book by Al Perkins. Random House, 1970. Noses are interesting and serve many purposes, including holding up glasses.

Noisy Breakfast by Ellen Blonder. Scholastic, 1994. Simple text allows you to listen as a dog and a mouse chow down.

Polar Bear, Polar Bear, What Do You Hear? by Bill Martin Jr. Henry Holt & Company, 1991. Zoo animals from polar bear to walrus make their distinctive sounds for each other, while the children imitate the sounds for the zookeeper.

The Quiet Noisy Book by Margaret Wise Brown. HarperCollins, 1993 (reissue). A little dog named Muffin is awakened by a tiny noise that sends him on a search to find out what it is.

Rosa's Parrot by Jan Wahl. Whispering Coyote Press, 1999. When Rosa has trouble hearing, her parrot sometimes repeats things for her properly, and sometimes creates mischief.

Sense Suspense: A Guessing Game For the Five Senses by Bruce McMillan. Scholastic, 1994. A concept game presented in book format in both English and Spanish. Young readers discover what's pictured in the mysterious photographs as well as figure out which senses they are most likely to use as two island youngsters take them on a sunny Caribbean sense-adventure.

Sight by María Rius. Barron's, 1985. Text and illustrations present a variety of pleasant sights. Included is a short scientific explanation of our sense of sight, with a diagram of the eye.

Slop Goes the Soup: A Noisy Warthog Word Book by Pamela Duncan Edwards. Hyperion, 2001. When warthog sneezes while carrying soup to the table, he begins an onomatopoeic chain reaction that involves the whole family.

Smell by María Rius. Barron's, 1985. Text and illustrations present interesting smells. Included is a short scientific explanation of our sense of smell, with a diagram of the nose.

So Many Sounds by Dana Meachen Rau. Children's Press, 2001. Listen to the various sounds of people, animals, and a train. (The children can repeat the sounds as you read the story.)

Splish Splash Bang Crash! by Karen Gundersheimer. Cartwheel, 1995. Pictures and brief rhyming text depict a group of children having noisy fun at play.

Summer Noisy Book by Margaret Wise Brown. HarperCollins, 1993 (reissue). On a trip to the country, a little dog named Muffin encounters all kinds of new and puzzling sounds.

Taste by María Rius. Barron's, 1985. Text and illustrations present things that taste sweet, sour, salty, delicious, and terrible. Included is a picture of the tongue and a short explanation of our sense of taste.

Touch by María Rius. Barron's, 1985. Text and illustrations present a variety of things to be felt with the skin. Included is a short scientific explanation of our sense of touch, with a diagram of a section of skin.

The Very Noisy Night by Diana Hendry. Dutton Children's Books, 1999. Little Mouse is frightened by all the different sounds he hears at bedtime, but Big Mouse always knows just what that sound is.

What Does Baby Hear? by Denise Lewis Patrick and Kathy Cruickshank. Golden Books, 1990. Explore the sounds a baby might hear. (Have the children make the sounds as you tell the story.)

What Noises Can You Hear? by Hannah Reidy. Zero to Ten Limited, 1999. Examines the sounds heard during the course of the day, from an alarm clock to the kitchen, street, and playground, to an owl outside the window at night.

What's that Awful Smell? by Heather Tekavec. Dial, 2004. While investigating an odor in their barn, a group of animals discovers a little piglet and engages in a variety of antics to get rid of the awful smell.

What Was That! by Geda Bradley Matthews. Goldencraft, 1985. Three skittish brothers try to comfort each other when they hear night noises in their house.

You Can't Taste a Pickle With Your Ear by Harriet Ziefert. Blue Apple Books, 2002. Introduces the five senses with comical illustrations and rhyming text, which could be used for storytime. Introduce the facts in each chapter as a means for discussion. There are questions listed at the end of every chapter that are also helpful.

Additional Resources

Video

Our Five Senses. 1997. 12 minutes. 100% Educational Videos, Inc. 4921 Robert J. Mathews Parkway, Suite 2 El Dorado Hills, Ca 95762 Phone: 1-800-483-3383 Fax: 1-888-478-1426 www.schoolvideos.com

Name Tag Patterns for Our Sensational Senses

My Five Senses Face Patterns

My Five Senses Face Patterns

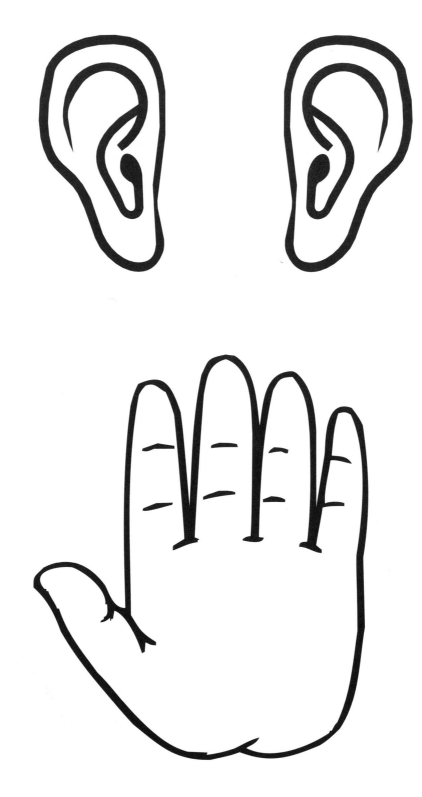

Silly Dilly Tales
Opposites, Humorous Stories, Imagination

Before Storytime

Name Tags

Copy the name tags on pages 135–136. Make enough copies so you have one name tag per child; cut out and list each child's name. You may wish to pin each name tag on with a safety pin, copy the name tags onto removable adhesive paper, or punch a hole in the top of each name tag and string it with yarn for a necklace.

Props

Wear clothes that do not match, a shirt backwards, shoes on the wrong feet, or two different kinds of shoes.

Storytime

- Introduce the theme by asking the children about their name tags.

- Show props and ask questions such as, "Do I look silly?" "I feel very silly today!" "Why do you think I look silly?"

- Sing the storytime song on page 10.

- Intersperse stories, songs, fingerplays, and activities that fit within your time frame.

Snack

- Offer pickles and ice cream (they will probably only take you up on one, but you never know!).

- Serve the drink for the day with silly straws. To make your own silly straws, get clear, flexible tubing sold by the foot at hardware stores. It is already intended for consumption so no need to worry about washing it. Get the ⅜" or (if available) ¼" tubing, and tie a loose knot in it. You will need approximately 1' per straw.

Discussion Questions

Ask specific questions to reinforce comprehension concepts, re-ignite excitement for the stories shared, enrich children's vocabulary, and influence narrative skills.

For example:

- "Have you ever pretended to be some of the things Jillian Jiggs was in the story, *Jillian Jiggs*?" "Did you ever play with boxes like Jillian?" "What were some of the things Jillian and her friends pretended to be?"

- "Do you remember which animal got on the bus in *The Seals on the Bus* that scared them all off?"

- "Tell me some of the things they did to Imogene's antlers in *Imogene's Antlers.*"

- "What animal laughed so loud it was hard to hear the story in *I Took My Frog to the Library*?"

- "Name some of the opposite things mentioned in *The Good Little Bad Little Pig*?"

- Before reading *Pickles In My Soup,* pose the riddle, "What is green, sour, or sweet, that many of us love to eat?"

Wrapping It Up

Sing the song on page 11.

Songs

Opposites

Sung to the tune: "London Bridges"

Up and down are opposites,
Opposites, opposites.
Up and down are opposites.
Let's think of more.

Use the children's suggestions and act out each suggestion as best you can, such as touching your toes and raising your hands above your head.

Silly Wiggle

Sung to the tune: "The Farmer in the Dell"

A silly wiggle here,
A silly wiggle there,
Wiggle your fingers now,
Up in the air.

Now place them on the ground,
And wiggle them around.
We've got silly fingers up and down.

A silly wiggle here,
A silly wiggle there,
Wiggle your knees,
And your derriere!

Wiggle them round and round,
And up and down.

We got the sillies,
When we went to town.
Now we better sit down,
Oh don't you frown—
Turn that frown back upside down! *(Smile!)*

Do Your Ears Hang Low?

Traditional

Do your ears hang low?
Do they wobble to and fro?
Can you tie them in a knot?
Can you tie them in a bow?
Can you throw them over your shoulder like a continental soldier?
Do your ears hang low?

Make You Smile

Sung to the tune: "Hokey Pokey"

We'll show how silly we can be,
As we move so happily.

Let's make a silly face,
Then move from place to place.
We'll all be silly for just a while.
That's how we'll make you smile!

Fingerplays

Over and Under

Author Unknown

Have children demonstrate, or use an object or your hand.

Over and under,
In front of, beside,
Inside and outside,
Are places to hide.
On and behind,
Among and between,
Are places to be,
Where I cannot be seen!

Father Bought a Feather Duster

Author Unknown

Father bought a feather duster, *(Pretend to use a feather duster, or display a real one.)*
Mother laid it down. *(Set it down.)*
Grandma sewed it to her hat, *(Pat head.)*
And wore it into town! *(Lift head proudly.)*

A Silly Monkey

Author Unknown

A silly little monkey,
(Place hands under arms, elbows out, and itch.)
Called me on the phone.
(Pretend to hold phone to ear.)
"Hello? Hello? Are you there alone?
(Place hand to ear.)
I'm a silly little monkey, *(Point to self.)*
Calling from the zoo. *(Pretend to dial a phone.)*
If you're very lonely, *(Point to children.)*
I'll come and visit you!"
(Point to self, then children.)

Soon that little monkey,
(Place hands under arms, elbows out, and itch.)
Was knocking on my door. *(Knock at a door.)*
And growing a banana tree,
(Place hands together and spread out over head.)
Right through my kitchen floor!
(Point to floor.)

Poems

The Purple Cow

Author Unknown

I never saw a purple cow.
I never hope to see one.
But I can tell you anyhow,
I'd rather see than be one!

I Had a Silly Day

Suggestion: Read before nap time.

I had a day, a silly day.
Everything went awry.
I thought that there must be something
Wrong with my eye!

For everything I saw,
Was backwards and upside down.
Everyone was walking
On the clouds in town!

A man was on a leash,
Walked by a dog.
And I thought I saw a car
Being driven by a frog!

I know I had my breakfast,
All mixed-up today.
I ate the jelly first
And then gave my toast away.

I put juice on my cereal,
And buttered the banana.
Put syrup in my milk
And called Dean, Deanna!

I knew it when I got up,
From the wrong side of the bed.
That this would be a day
I might soon dread.

So even though it's noon,
I think I'll go back to bed.
And put the pillows up
Over my head.

Maybe take a nap,
And try it in an hour.
Get up on the right side
And take a quick shower.

Then I'll be refreshed,
To start the day anew.
You might want to try it
For your silly days too!

Activities

Mixed Up Animals

Read Down on the Funny Farm *or* Old Mr. Mackle Hackle *and give the children their farm animals to color. Talk about the opposites (front, back, head, tail) involved with this silly coloring book.*

Supplies needed:

- animals on pages 133–134
- crayons/markers
- scissors
- paper
- yarn
- hole punch

Directions:

1. Copy the animals from pages 133–134 so every child has one of each animal. You will want to center each picture on the page and enlarge the animals so that they fill the page. Every animal should be approximately the same size.

2. Stack the pictures on top of each other and hole punch the sides of the pages so all of the holes line up.

3. String yarn through the holes to create a book.

4. Make a cut in the center of the book, cutting each animal in half. Leave about 1" uncut on the left edge to hold the pictures together.

5. After the children color the pictures they can flip the pages and create a mixed-up animal.

6. Encourage the children to name their new silly creature. Also encourage phonological awareness where they play with the sounds of words, and narration as they describe their creation.

Gross Motor Activities

Silly Dilly Dressing

Supplies needed:

- old clothes of all kinds

Directions:

1. Line the children up and place the clothes in a pile on the floor at the other end of the room.

2. One child at a time walks backwards to the clothes and puts everything on backwards, upside down, or inside out. Discuss those concepts.

Silly or Right?

Directions:

1. Everyone sits in a circle.

2. One person begins by saying a statement that is either correct or silly, such as "cows moo," "sheep meow," "trains float," "boats sail on train tracks," "bananas are yellow," or "French fries are made from dirt," etc.

3. When the children hear a silly statement they pat their heads while rubbing their tummies (or try to).

4. When they hear a statement that is right, they clap.

Math & Science Activity

Bubble-orb-ology

Supplies needed:

- soap bubbles

- bowl of water

- 2 paper clips

- a very small amount of vegetable oil

- soap bubble wands

- fork

Directions:

1. Ask the children if they think a paper clip will float or sink in a bowl of water. Drop the paper clip in the bowl. (It will sink.) Ask the children if they would like to see you float a paper clip in water.

2. Use a small amount of oil and rub it on the other paper clip.

3. Place the paper clip on the fork and place it in the water. It will float because the oil will create a thin "skin" on the water and support the paper clip.

4. Blow some bubbles in the air and ask if the children know why they are able to form bubbles.

5. Explain that the ingredients in soap bubbles are oily, causing the bubble mix to create a thin skin that can stretch. The more oil in the mix, the longer the bubble will last.

6. Ask the children if they see any color in the bubbles. You can sometimes see color when light hits the soap film (oil).

7. Blow one bubble at a time and have the children predict how long the bubble will last. Count out loud until the bubble pops.

8. Everyone blow bubbles!

Fine Motor Skills Activities

Puppet Stage

Supplies needed:

- any puppets you have available

- medium-sized box

- large scarf

- push pins

Directions:

1. Remove the top and bottom flaps from the box so all that remains is a frame.

2. Using push pins, tack a scarf on the top of the box and allow it to drape down for your stage curtain.

3. Place your "stage" on a table so the children can stand behind it to perform.

4. Encourage the children to have their puppets tell jokes, riddles, funny or silly stories and to really ham it up.

Backwards Drop

Supplies needed:

- clean plastic jar with a wide mouth

- unsharpened pencils

Directions:

1. Set the jar on the floor and have the children stand in front of it.

2. Have them drop a pencil into the opening of the jar.

3. Turn the children around and have them try it again from behind their backs.

Storytime Books to Share

Animals Should Definitely Not Act Like People by Judi Barrett. Atheneum, 1980. Pictures of animals wearing clothes show why this would be a ridiculous custom for them to adopt.

April Fool! by Harriet Ziefert. Puffin, 2000. On April 1, Will tells his friends how he once saw a bike-riding elephant that sang through his trunk while juggling six bags of junk.

April Foolishness by Teresa Bateman. Albert Whitman, 2004. Grandpa fixes his visiting grandkids breakfast while they try to trick him for April Fool's Day, but grandma has a surprise of her own.

Arthur in a Pickle by Marc Brown. Random House, 1999. After lying about what happened to his homework, Arthur has such a bad dream about being in a "pickle" that he decides to tell the truth.

Bad Hare Day by Miriam Moss. Bloomsbury Children's Books, 2003. Uncle Herbert the Hare, the best hairdresser in town, has his hands full when his niece Holly spends time at his salon.

Belly Button Boy by Peter Maloney. Puffin, 2000. After neglecting to bathe, Billy is surprised to find that a bush is growing from his dirt-filled belly button.

Cloudy with a Chance of Meatballs by Judi Barrett. Atheneum, 1978. Life is delicious in the town of Chewandswallow where it rains soup and juice, snows mashed potatoes, and blows storms of hamburgers—until the weather takes a turn for the worse.

Dancing Granny by Elizabeth Winthrop. Marshall Cavendish, 2003. Granny and her grandchild take a nighttime trip to the zoo, where the animals have prepared a fabulous party and Granny dances the night away.

The Day the Dog Dressed Like Dad by Tom Amico and James Proimos. Bloomsbury Publishing, 2004. One day when dad is out of town, the family dog decides to take over his role by demanding some grub, taking the family on a picnic, and hogging the remote.

Don't Laugh, Joe by Keiko Kasza. Putnam, 1997. Mother Possum is in despair because her son cannot learn to play dead without laughing.

Down On The Funny Farm by P. E. King. Random House, 1986. A farmer thinks he is getting a bargain when he buys a farm for one dollar, until he finds that all the animals are mixed up about what they are supposed to do.

Drat that Fat Cat! by Pat Thomson. Arthur A. Levine, 2003. A fat cat in search of food eats up everything he meets until he swallows a bee.

The Flea's Sneeze by Lynn Downey. Henry Holt & Company, 2000. A flea with a cold startles all the animals in the barn when it sneezes unexpectedly.

George Upside Down by Meghan McCarthy. Viking, 2003. After George starts doing everything upside down, his parents and teacher do the same and so he must think of something new.

Imogene's Antlers by David Small. Dragonfly Books, 1985. One Thursday Imogene wakes up with a pair of antlers growing out of her head and causes a sensation wherever she goes.

I Took My Frog to the Library by Eric A. Kimmel. Puffin, 1990. A young girl brings her pets to the library with disastrous results.

Jillian Jiggs by Phoebe Gilman. Scholastic, 1985. Jillian Jiggs is a little girl who hates to clean her room. She promises her mother she will clean it, but her imagination gets the best of her when her friends come over.

Let's Go Swimming with Mr. Sillypants by M. K. Brown. Crown Publishers, 1986. Mr. Sillypants worries so much about his swimming lesson that he has a dream in which he turns into a fish.

Make Way for Dumb Bunnies by Sue Denim. Blue Sky Press, 1996. The Dumb Bunnies have a very active day, during which they do many things backwards or wrong.

Mixed-up Mother Goose by Leonard Kessler. Leonard Kessler, 1980. Mother Goose plans a party for all her nursery rhyme friends but on her way home with the party things, she falls and becomes mixed-up.

More Parts by Tedd Arnold. Dial, 2001. A young boy is worried about what will happen to his body when he hears such expressions as "give him a hand" and "hold your tongue."

Mr. Reez's Sneezes by Curtis Parkinson. Scholastic, 1999. Mr. Reeze was a quiet man, until he sneezes! While sprinkling pepper on his salad he sneezes and many silly things happen, leaving Mr. Reeze to decide he likes his quiet life.

Mrs. McNosh Hangs Up Her Wash by Sarah Weeks. Harper Trophy, 1998. Mrs. McNosh's wash is certainly big—and definitely wacky—as the day goes on things get even sillier.

Mrs. Piggle-Wiggle's Won't-Pick-Up-Toys Cure by Betty MacDonald. HarperCollins, 1975. Mrs. Piggle-Wiggle suggests a cure for Hubert's bad habit of not picking up his toys.

My Little Sister Ate One Hare by Bill Grossman. Crown Books, 1996. Little sister has no problem eating one hare, two snakes, and three ants, but when she gets to ten peas, she throws up quite a mess.

No Laughing, No Smiling, No Giggling by James Stevenson. Farrar, Straus and Giroux, 2004. The reader joins Freddy Fafnaffer the pig as he deals with Mr. Frimdimpny, a crocodile who never laughs and who decides on the rules for reading this book.

Old Mr. Mackle Hackle by Gunnar Madsen. Little, Brown and Company, 2005. Old Mr. Mackle Hackle is concerned when his hen will not cackle, so he takes her to a doctor and a fortune-teller, and even tries telling her chicken jokes, but once her chicks are hatched the tables are turned.

One Windy Wednesday by Phyllis Root. Candlewick Press, 1996. When the wind blows so hard that it blows the quack right out of the duck, the oink right out of the pig, and so on, Bonnie Bumble works hard to get each animal's sound back where it belongs.

Oops! by Colin McNaughton. Harcourt, 1997. A confused wolf and a clumsy pig named Preston meet in a story that combines elements of "Little Red Riding Hood" and "The Three Little Pigs."

Parts by Tedd Arnold. Dial, 1997. A five-year-old boy thinks his body is falling apart until he learns new teeth grow, and hair and skin replace themselves.

Pickles in My Soup by Mary Pearson. Children's Press, 1999. A girl loves to eat pickles in all kinds of unusual combinations.

Pickle Things by Marc Brown. Parents Magazine Press, 1990. Describes in rhyme the many things a pickle isn't.

The Seals on the Bus by Lenny Hort. Scholastic, 2000. Based on the song "The Wheels on the Bus," this story uses animals with a surprise ending when the skunks arrive.

Sheep in a Jeep by Nancy Shaw. Houghton Mifflin, 1986. A flock of hapless sheep drive through the country in this rhyming picture book.

Sheep Out to Eat by Nancy Shaw. Houghton Mifflin, 1992. Five hungry sheep discover that a teashop may not be the best place for them to eat.

The Silly Mother Hubbard by Leonard Kessler. Garrard Publishing Co., 1980. In this take-off of the well known Mother Hubbard rhyme, Mother Hubbard goes to extraordinary lengths to make her dog happy.

Silly Sally by Audrey Wood. Harcourt, 1992. A rhyming story of Silly Sally, who makes many friends as she travels to town—backwards and upside down.

Silly Sara by Anna Jane Hays. Random House, 2002. Alliterative rhyming tale of a girl who can be very silly but with her best friend, Sam, she discovers she can be something more.

The Silly Tail Book by Marc Brown. Parents Magazine Press, 1983. Explains, in rhymed text and illustrations, what tails are and aren't, what they can and can't do, and where they do and don't grow.

Silly Willy by Maryann Cocca-Leffler. Grosset & Dunlap, 1995. Willy's silliness while dressing—putting gloves on his feet and shoes on his hands—amuses his big sister. A rebus book that comes with flash cards.

Skeleton Hiccups by Margery Cuyler. Margaret K. McElderry Books, 2002. Ghost tries to help Skeleton get rid of his hiccups.

Smile a Lot by Nancy Carlson. Carolrhoda Books, 2002. A frog explains how smiling is a great way to get through life's ups and downs.

Stinky Smelly Feet by Margie Palatini. Dutton Children's Books, 2004. When stinky feet threaten the romance between Douglas and Dolores, they must find a solution.

The Stupids Step Out by Harry Allard. Houghton Mifflin, 1974. The Stupids and their dog, Kitty, have a fun-filled day doing ridiculous things.

That's Not All! by Rex Schneider. School Zone Publishing, 1992. A woman has a strange start to her day and it gets stranger as the day goes on. With no way for the day to end, she joins in the fun.

There's a Wocket in my Pocket by Dr. Seuss. Random House, 1974. Silly rhyming words describe many items in a house.

Tumble Bumble by Felicia Bond. Front Street, 1996. A tiny bug goes for a walk, but it's no ordinary stroll. Soon he bumps into a cat, then a crocodile, and even a baby pig! More creatures join in, until they tippy-toe into a mysterious yellow house belonging to a young boy, who happily tumble bumbles right along with them.

The Turn-Around Upside-Down Alphabet Book by Lisa Campbell Ernst. Simon & Schuster, 2004. Every letter of the alphabet becomes three different objects as the book is turned in different directions. A fun and imaginative way to learn the alphabet.

Turnover Tuesday by Phyllis Root. Candlewick Press, 1998. When Bonnie Bumble eats five plum turnovers for breakfast one morning her whole world is turned upside down.

Two Crazy Pigs by Karen Berman Nagel. Cartwheel, 1992. Two pigs who drive the farmer and his wife crazy with their silliness and pranks decide to move to a new farm, only to be missed by all the other animals when they leave.

Wacky Wednesday by Theodore LeSieg. Random House, 1974. Drawings and verse point out the many things that are wrong one wacky Wednesday when a youngster awakens to find everything out of place, but no one else notices.

Opposites

Alien Opposites by Matthew Van Fleet. Hyperion, 2000. When an unruly gang of aliens visits the home of a little boy, what follows is a night of fun, mischief, and opposites.

America: A Book of Opposites by W. Nikola-Lisa. Lee & Low, 2001. Illustrated by ten talented and ethnically varied children's book artists, this new edition celebrates in words (both Spanish and English) and images what America is all about—diversity. Young children are led through a land of opposites, where they learn how to differentiate between high and low, wet and dry, and rough and smooth.

Beach Is to Fun: A Book of Relationships by Pat Brisson. Henry Holt & Company, 2004. A vibrant picture book that presents clever, rhyming analogies to help children learn the connections between words and their meanings. The colorful illustrations feature a boy, a girl, and their dog enjoying a variety of summer activities.

The Bear and the Fly by Paula Winter. Crown, 1976. A bear tries to catch a fly with disastrous results. This wordless picture book is great for promoting narrative skills.

Build It Up and Knock It Down by Tom Hunter and James Yang. Harper Festival, 2002. Teaches about opposites and how to make friends.

Fortunately by Remy Charlip. Aladdin, 1993. Fortunately, Ned was invited to a surprise party. Unfortunately, the party was a thousand miles away. What goes wrong as Ned tries to get to the party? Readers will cheer as Ned's luck turns from good to bad to good again, while clever illustrations tell the story of his wacky adventure and narrow escapes.

The Good Little Bad Little Pig by Margaret Wise Brown. Hyperion, 2002. A boy's wish comes true when he gets a little pet pig that is sometimes good and sometimes bad.

How Big is a Pig by Stella Blackstone. Barefoot Books, 2000. Follow the trail of animal opposites through the farmyard as it leads you to the biggest pig of all.

Olivia's Opposites by Ian Falconer. Atheneum, 2002. She's up, she's down, she's plain, and she's fancy. Keep up with busy Olivia as she changes her mind about everything.

Opposites by Chuck Murphy. Simon & Schuster, 2001. A "slide 'n' seek" book that uses bright, simple illustrations to convey basic opposite concepts.

Opposites with Oswald by Lauryn Silverhardt. Simon Spotlight, 2003. Learn the difference between hot and cold, up and down, and more along with Oswald.

Roger's Upside-Down Day by Betty Ren Wright. Goldencraft, 1979. Roger woke up feeling funny. In this rhyming story Roger's day gets even stranger with everything happening opposite of what it should.

Snappy Little Opposites by Dugald Steer. Millbrook Press, 2000. Enjoy the ins and outs of opposites in this colorful, fun book that shows big and small, asleep and awake, and more.

That's Good! That's Bad! by Margery Cuyler. Henry Holt & Company, 1991. A little boy has a series of adventures and misadventures with a bunch of wild animals.

Ten Dirty Pigs; Ten Clean Pigs: An Upside-Down, Turn-Around Bathtime Counting Book by Carol Roth. North-South Books, 1999. In rhyming stories printed back to back, pigs from one to ten take baths to clean up and then get dirty again.

To & Fro, Fast & Slow by Durga Bernhard. Walker & Co., 2001. A girl who is shuttled between the homes of her divorced parents observes such opposites as "over, under," "rainy, sunny," and "full, empty."

Too Big, Too Small, Just Right by Frances Minters. Harcourt, 2000. Two rabbits searching for a new home encounter such opposites as big and small, short and tall, and heavy and light.

Patterns for Mixed Up Animals Activity

Patterns for Mixed Up Animals Activity

Patterns for Mixed Up Animals Activity

Stargazing
Stars & Planets, Space Travel, Astronauts

Before Storytime

Name Tags

Copy the name tags on page 145. Make enough copies so you have one name tag per child; cut out and list each child's name. You may wish to pin each name tag on with a safety pin, copy the name tags onto removable adhesive paper, or punch a hole in the top of each name tag and string it with yarn for a necklace.

Props

- Take a wide brimmed hat and place stars, comets, and planets on it. Use double-sided tape or tape the items to the ends of fishing line so they hang down at various lengths. Face-paint stars and moons on your cheek.

- If you would like to be an astronaut, wear blue jumpsuits with the American flag and the NASA logo on them when in training.

- For aliens I think you can be as creative as you want and no one can argue!

Storytime

- Introduce the theme by asking the children about their name tags.

- Show props and ask questions such as, "Where would I be going if I look like this?" "Who do you think I am pretending to be?"

- Sing the storytime song on page 10.

- Intersperse stories, songs, fingerplays, and activities that fit within your time frame.

Snack
Astronaut food

- Talk to the children about how everything astronauts eat is in a tube or a bag because that is the only way their food will not float away.

Smoothies

Supplies needed:

- fresh fruit
- blender
- orange juice
- straws
- zipper sandwich bags

Directions:

1. Mix the fruit and juice in a blender.
2. Pour into a zipper bag.
3. Give each child a bag and a straw.
4. Serve Jell-O made in star shapes with your smoothies.

Discussion Questions

Ask specific questions to reinforce comprehension concepts, re-ignite excitement for the stories shared, enrich children's vocabulary, and influence narrative skills.

For example:

- "Who told Stella all about the stars in *Stella Princess of the Sky*?"

- "Did Sydney's star turn out to be useful, in the book *Sydney's Star*?"

- "Where did the boy walk with the moon in *I Took the Moon for a Walk*?"

- "What was the thing from outer space mistaken for in *Space Case*?"

- "Why were the slaves able to make it to Canada in *Follow the Drinking Gourd?*"

Wrapping It Up

Sing the song on page 11.

Songs

Off We Go

Sung to the tune: "Frére Jacques"

Do as an echo.

Here's the rocket, here's the rocket,
Get aboard! Get aboard!
We'll all blast off; we'll all blast off,
Into space! Into space! (*Crouch down and do sound effects.*)

Climb Aboard the Spaceship

Author Unknown

Sung to the tune: "The Eensy Weensy Spider"

Climb aboard the spaceship,
We're going to the moon.
Hurry and get ready,
We're going to blast off soon.

Put on your helmets.
And buckle up real tight.
Here comes the countdown,
Let's count with all our might.
10–9–8–7–6–5–4–3–2–1!—BLAST OFF!

We're Flying

Author Unknown

Sung to the tune: "The Farmer in the Dell"

We're flying to the moon,
We're flying to the moon,
Blast off, away we go,
We're flying to the moon.

Other verses:

We're going on the shuttle ...

We're walking out in space ...

We're landing on the moon ...

We're collecting moon rocks ...

We're flying back to Earth ...

A Star Makes an Excellent Night-light

Author Unknown

Sung to the tune: "My Bonnie Lies Over the Ocean"

A star makes an excellent night-light,
A star keeps the moon company.
A star when it twinkles is so bright.
Oh star won't you twinkle for me?

Twinkle, twinkle, oh twinkle your bright light for me, for me.
Twinkle, twinkle, oh twinkle your bright light for me!

When I'm Lying in My Bed

Author Unknown

Sung to the tune: "The Ants Go Marching In"

When I'm lying in my bed at night,
At night, at night.
The moon shines down from overhead,
So bright, so bright.

When I am lying in my bed,
The moon shines down from overhead.
And it makes my room so light, at night,
With its bright moonlight.

I See

Sung to the tune: "He's Got the Whole World in His Hands"

I see lots of stars, in the sky,
I see lots of stars, in the sky,
I see lots of stars, in the sky,
Twinkling at you and me!

I see the full moon shinin' in the sky,
I see the full moon shinin' in the sky,
I see the full moon shinin' in the sky,
It's shinin' 'round you and me!

I see a comet go flying right on by,
I see a comet go flying right on by,
I see a comet go flying right on by,
It flies right on in the sky.

We're Going to Outer Space

Sung to the tune: "The Farmer in the Dell"

We're going to outer space,
We're going to outer space.
Wow! Look, it's such a big, big, big place!

There's stars and planets there,
Just hanging in mid air.
Comets flying 'round the sun,
Won't it be such fun?

Let's start off at the moon,
Our shuttle leaves soon.
Let's go all the way,
To the Milky Way!

Action Songs

Climb Aboard the Spaceship

Author Unknown

Sung to the tune: "The Eensy Weensy Spider"

Climb aboard the spaceship,
(Pretend to climb aboard.)
We're going to the moon.
Hurry and get ready, *(Pretend to dress.)*
We're going to blast off soon!

Put on your helmets, *(Pretend to put on helmet.)*
And buckle up real tight. *(Pretend to buckle up.)*
Here comes the countdown, *(Crouch down.)*
Let's count with all our might ...
10–9–8–7–6–5–4–3–2–1!—BLAST OFF!
(Jump up.)

Ring Around the Rocket Ship

Author Unknown

Sung to the tune: "Ring Around the Rosie"

Ring around the rocket ship,
Try to grab a star.
Stardust, stardust,
Fall where you are!

Fingerplays

Blast off

Author Unknown

Rocket headed for the moon, *(Point upward.)*
Astronauts are coming soon. *(Walk stiffly.)*
Buttons to push—there's a bunch, *(Push buttons.)*
Don't forget to pack your lunch. *(Rub stomach.)*
5–4–3–2–1 *(Squat low with each number.)*
Blast off! *(Jump up.)*

Stars

Author Unknown

The stars you see at night, *(Point upward.)*
Are like our sun, so warm and bright.
*(Place fingers together in a circle and shade eyes
with other hand while looking up.)*
But far away, they look so small, *(Stretch arm
out; place index and pointer finger together.)*
They barely give us light at all.
(Open eyes widely, strain to see the stars.)

Four Little Stars

Author Unknown

Four little stars winking at me.
(Hold up appropriate fingers.)
One shot off and now there are three!
(Move one finger away and hide hand.)

Three little stars with nothing to do.
(Hold up appropriate fingers.)
One shot off and now there are two!
(Move one finger away and hide hand.)

Two little stars afraid of the sun.
(Hold up appropriate fingers.)
One shot off now there is one!
(Move one finger away and hide hand.)

One little star alone is no fun.
(Hold up appropriate fingers.)
It shot off and now there are none!
(Move one finger away and hide hand.)

Five Little Astronauts

Author Unknown

Five little astronauts headed for the moon.
(Hold up hand; wiggle all fingers.)

The first one said, "I hope we get there
soon." *(Wiggle thumb.)*

The second one said, "I think I see a star."
(Wiggle first finger.)

The third one said, "I wonder where we are."
(Wiggle middle finger.)

The fourth one said, "We're just about to
land." *(Wiggle ring finger.)*

The fifth one said, "Isn't this just grand?"
(Wiggle pinky finger.)

Five little astronauts looked all around.
(Hold up hand; wiggle all fingers.)

Then off they soared, until they reached the ground. (*Move hand up in the air and land down.*)

Go to the Moon

Author Unknown

Do you want to go up with me to the moon?
(*Point to children.*)
Let's get in our rocket ship,
(*Pretend to climb aboard.*)
And blast off soon! (*Bend down and jump up.*)

Faster and faster, we reach the sky.
(*Stretch high on toes and reach arms over head.*)
Isn't it fun to be able to fly?

We're on the moon, (*Stand and look around.*)
Now all take a look. (*Continue to look.*)
And gently sit down, (*Sit down.*)
While I show you a book.
(*Point to children; make the sign language sign for book by placing your hands in prayer and opening them wide while your little fingers remain touching.*)

Zoom, Zoom, Zoom

Author Unknown

Zoom, zoom, zoom,
(*Place hands together like praying; swish upward.*)
We're going to the moon!
(*Make a circle with hands in the air.*)

If you want to take a trip, (*Point to children.*)
Climb aboard my rocket ship.
(*Beckon with hand.*)

Zoom, zoom, zoom,
(*Place hands together like praying; swish upward.*)
We're going to the moon!
(*Make a circle with hands in the air.*)

10–9–8–7–6–5–4–3–2–1!—BLAST OFF!
(*Crouch down as you count and jump up.*)

Activities

Sparkly Stars

After reading *Sydney's Star* by Peter Reynolds, help the children make sparkly stars while singing "Twinkle Twinkle, Little Star."

Supplies needed:

- yarn

- glitter glue*, glitter, or cornmeal

- markers

- sequins and/or aluminum foil

- hole punch

Directions:

1. Cut out the stars from the pattern on page 145.

2. Have the children decorate with markers, sequins, glitter (glitter glue can be a bit neater to use), or white cornmeal (cosmic dust).

3. Punch a hole in the top and place a piece of yarn through the hole, allowing for the star to hang.

   * To make your own glitter glue, use disposable individual containers with lids (you might try asking at sandwich shops or delis), add glue and glitter and stir with a Popsicle stick.

Alien Flying Space Ship

After reading *Hush Little Alien* or *Space Case* make your own alien space ship.

Supplies needed:

- paper plate (1 per child)

- paper or Styrofoam coffee cup (1 per child)

- flexible straws

- scrap construction paper

- scissors

- markers

- sharpened pencil

- tape

- stickers or rubber stamps, stamp pad (*optional*)

Directions:

1. In the center of the paper plate, trace around the wide end (top) of the drinking cup.

2. Cut out the traced portion. The wide end of the cup should fit through the plate.

3. Have the children fit their cup through the hole, holding the cup upside down and feeding it up through the bottom. The narrow end should face the top.

4. Use the sharpened pencil to poke a hole on either side of the narrow end of the cup.

5. Have the children cut out two eyes from the scrap construction paper.

6. Have them use markers to draw eyeballs onto their eye shapes.

7. Stick a straw through each hole, leaving the flexible end exposed at the top.

8. Tape the eyeballs to the bent ends of the straws.

9. Decorate the space ship.

10. To fly, throw the space ship like you would a flying disk, holding the edge of the plate and tossing sideways with your wrist.

Rockets

Supplies needed:

- paper towel tube (or toilet paper tube for smaller rockets)
- construction paper
- markers
- star stickers
- tape
- scissors

Directions:

1. Cut a piece of construction paper 4¼" x 4½" and roll into a cone shape. Tape the edges together to hold the cone shape.

2. Use the scissors to even off the bottom of the cone so it can stand flush on a table. This will enable it to sit inside the tube.

3. Place the tip of the cone into the paper tube to create the top of the rocket. The pointed end of the cone should project up and through the end of the tube.

4. Secure the edge of the cone to the inside of the paper towel tube with a ring of glue around the outer edge.

5. Cut a circle from construction paper approximately 4" in diameter.

6. Cut your circle in half and in half again, making four equal pieces.

7. To create the rocket's fins, tape the pieces to the bottom of the tube around the sides, or cut four 2" slits into the tube and slide the paper into the slits.

8. Decorate the tubes with markers and stickers, and blast off!

Space Shuttle

Directions:

To create a space shuttle, follow the above directions, but place the paper towel tube on its side instead of standing upright.

1. Trace the end of the paper towel tube on a small piece of thin cardboard.

2. Cut around the circle just to the outside making it slightly larger than the paper towel tube end.

3. Block one end of the tube with the cut cardboard by gluing it to one end of the paper towel tube.

4. Cut ½" strips out of black construction paper about 1½" long. Roll and attach to the covered end of the tube for the rocket booster engines.

5. Cut two wings from construction paper approximately 2" at the base and 4" from the bottom to the tip.

6. Attach the wings at the top and bottom.

You may wish to discuss the similarities and differences between the rocket and the space shuttle, and why we use one and not the other any longer—the top used to disengage, and now it is part of the cockpit.

Gross Motor Activity

Hot Planet

Supplies needed:

- small red ball
- music

Suggestion: "Twinkle, Twinkle" on the CD *Jazz-a-ma-tazz* by Hayes Greenfield. Baby Music Boom, 1998.

Directions:

1. Everyone sits in a circle on the floor.

2. Explain that the red ball represents the planet Mars, which is very hot.

3. Pass the ball around quickly until the music stops.

4. Whomever is holding "Mars" when the music stops gets "shuttled" back home to Earth so they go in the center of the circle.

Math & Science Activities

Count the Stars

Supplies needed:

- star confetti
- baby food jar with lid (junior size) *
- water with blue food coloring added

Directions:

1. Place the colored water in the baby food jar so it is about three-quarters full.

2. Add some confetti.

3. After shaking the jar, ask the children if they can count the stars.

4. Explain that there really are so many stars in the universe that it would be this difficult to count the stars.

   * If you use the smaller baby food jars, this makes a nice space "snow" globe for the children to take home. You do need to tape around the lid with the clear, wide packing tape.

Gravity/Anti-Gravity

Supplies needed:

- ping-pong ball
- bowl of water
- table

Directions:

1. Explain that gravity keeps people and objects pulled towards the ground on Earth.

2. Place a ping-pong ball on a table. Talk about how even though it may roll (because it is round) it still stays on the table.

3. Place the ping-pong ball in water. Discuss how the water is like space, which has no gravity to hold us down; in space, we would float.

4. Push the ping-pong ball down into the water. Tell how gravity works like a weight pushing us to the ground, just like you are pushing the ping-pong ball down in the water.

5. Discuss how in space the astronauts weigh themselves down to walk on the moon.

6. Describe how in space when all of the weight is lifted (lift your hand off the ping-pong ball), we go back to anti- (which means no) gravity, and we float.

7. Allow the children to try different ways to experiment with anti-gravity. Will blowing on the ping-pong ball be enough to weigh it down? Why or why not? Try a light touch. How much force do we need to get it weighed down? Will it stay? Why or why not?

Many learning skills are being developed during this experiment, not only the scientific learning aspects, but the language and pre-reading skills of dialogic thinking and enriched vocabulary.

Fine Motor Skills Activities

My Own Universe

Supplies needed:

- star stickers in various colors
- paper
- markers/crayons

Directions:

1. Give the children the star stickers to peel off and place on their paper.

2. Have them create their own planets, Milky Way, and solar system.

3. Ask the children to count only one color at a time, and tell you which color of stars there are more of. Then have them point to the stars and count how many they put in their "universe."

Comets

Supplies needed:

- Jell-O mix (blue)
- paper

- spray bottle with water
- crayons

Directions:

1. Use crayons to create an outer space scene, leaving space for a comet to come through (white space where no crayons were used).

2. Sprinkle some Jell-O onto the "white space" of the picture.

3. Give the children spray bottles filled with water to spray at the Jell-O and create a shooting star effect.

Comet Facts:

1. Comets go around the sun.

2. Comets are made of ice, dust, and rock.

3. Comets are leftover from the cold, outer places far off in space.

4. We see the tail of comets because the sun shines on the dust.

Celestial Celebration

Using the face paint recipe on page 56, allow the children to have a small amount of face paint to make stars and moons on their hands, wrists, or cheeks (with a mirror).

Storytime Books to Share

Astro Bunnies by Christine Loomis. Putnam, 2001. Astro Bunnies rocket into space, explore, and return home.

Astronaut Piggy Wiggy by Christyan and Diane Fox. Handprint Books, 2002. Piggy Wiggy dreams of being an astronaut. Along with his faithful companion, Teddy, he boards a rocket dressed in his special space suit and blasts off to explore the wonders of the planets.

The Birthday Moon by Lois Duncan. Viking, 1989. Relates the wonderful things you can do with the perfect birthday gift—the moon.

The Boy who Ate the Moon by Christopher King. Philomel Books, 1988. After eating the moon, a boy takes a strange journey.

Coyote in Love With a Star by Marty Kreipe de Montaño. Abbeville Press, 1998. Coyote is a trickster character found in the stories of many Native American peoples. In this tale,

he leaves his home on a Potawatomi reservation on the Plains to find work in New York City. Once there, he falls in love with a star and leaves the earth to dance with her.

Coyote Places the Stars by Harriet Peck Taylor. Aladdin, 1997. In this Wasco Indian legend about the origin of the constellations, a clever coyote dreams big and confidently pursues his understanding of the heavens. First he builds a ladder to the moon. Then, being skilled with a bow, he shoots arrows at certain stars, moving them into the shapes of his animal friends.

Five Wishing Stars by Treesha Runnells. Piggy Toes Press, 2003. Five little sheep make a wish on glowing stars.

Follow the Drinking Gourd by Jeanette Winter. Knopf, 1988. Five slaves make it to Canada following the stars.

Here in Space by David Milgrim. Bridgewater Books, 1997. An imaginative young "space explorer" describes the many fascinating features of his home on the planet Earth.

How the Rabbit Stole the Moon by Louise Moeri. Houghton Mifflin, 1977. Tells the story of how a rabbit stole part of the sun and created the moon and stars.

How to Make a Night by Linda Ashman. HarperCollins, 2004. After a hectic day, it is time to bring on the night so that a child and her family can finally rest.

Hush, Little Alien by Daniel Kirk. Hyperion, 1999. In this adaptation of the old lullaby, "Hush Little Baby," an extraterrestrial child is promised an assortment of outer space presents, ending with a good night kiss from his adoring father.

I Took the Moon for a Walk by Carolyn Curtis and Alison Jay. Barefoot Books, 2004. A boy takes the moon for a walk through his neighborhood.

I Want to Be an Astronaut by Byron Barton. Harper Festival, 1988. This simple text reveals what it's like to be an astronaut in space.

Little Star adapted by Sarah Willson. Simon Spotlight, 2002. Dora the Explorer and Boots try to get Little Star home after a comet knocks him out of the sky.

Look at the Moon by May Garelick. Young Scott Books, 1969. Find out whether the moon shines everywhere as well as here as you visit night all over the world.

Me and My Place in Space by Joan Sweeney. Crown Books, 1998. A child describes how the earth, sun, and planets are part of our solar system, which is just one small part of the universe.

Moo Cow Kaboom! by Thacher Hurd. HarperCollins, 2003. One night, while the pigs and chickens are sound asleep—KABOOM!—Farmer George's Moo Cow disappears! A low-down Space Cowboy has whisked her off to a galaxy far, far away. What's this sweet cow to do now, forced to become the Wild Beast Earthling Moo Cow at the Inter-Galactic Rodeo?

The Moon Comes Home by Mary Jo Salter. Knopf, 1989. On the trip home by car from grandmother's house, a young child observes the moon.

The Moon Ring by Randy DuBurke. Chronicle Books, 2002. One hot night, Maxine goes on a wild adventure, thanks to the magic of the blue moon.

Rocket by Mick Inkpen. Red Wagon Books, 2001. When Kipper and Tiger launch a remote-controlled rocket with Sock Thing as the astronaut, they wonder if they will ever see Sock Thing again.

Space Case by Edward Marshall. Dial, 1980. When the thing from outer space visits Earth, it is taken first for a trick-or-treater and then for a robot.

Space Race by Judith Bauer Stamper. Scholastic, 1998. Zip, Zat, Zing, and Ray have a fun race in space. Includes related phonics activities.

Stella Princess of the Sky by Marie-Louise Gay. Groundwood Books, 2004. A vast luminous sky, the sun, the stars and the rising moon form the backdrop for Stella and her brother Sam's adventure, and as always, Stella has all the answers.

The Sun is My Favorite Star by Frank Asch. Gulliver Books, 2000. There are many stars in the galaxy. But only the sun wakes us in the morning, helps us to grow, plays hide-and-seek behind the clouds, and paints pretty pictures in the evening sky.

Sydney's Star by Peter Reynolds. Simon & Schuster, 2001. The malfunction of Sydney's mechanical star leads her to an unexpected happy ending.

Tinker and Tom and the Star Baby by David McPhail. Little, Brown and Company, 1998. Tinker and Tom, a boy and bear, find a Star Baby in their backyard and try to fix its spaceship so that it can return to its mother.

Twinkle, Twinkle, Little Star by Sylvia Long. Chronicle Books, 2001. The traditional lullaby is told in its entirety, as the poetic images celebrate the star appearing when the sun sets, guiding the traveler in the dark, glowing throughout the night, and remaining always mysterious.

Twinkle, Twinkle, Little Star by Jeanette Winter. Red Wagon Books, 2000. The classic lullaby is illustrated with simple yet evocative pictures as a little girl climbs a ladder to see what exactly the stars are and gathers one for herself.

What the Sun Sees/What the Moon Sees by Nancy Tafuri. Greenwillow Books, 1997. Contrasts the world as viewed in sunlight and then in the quiet night world in moonlight.

Who Gets the Sun Out of Bed? by Nancy White Carlstrom. Little, Brown and Company, 1992. In the cold, dark winter, the lazy sun is reluctant to rise, until the moon coaxes several members of a cozy household to get up.

Additional Resources

Visit **education.nasa.gov/home/index.html** for NASA educational resources.

Name Tag Patterns for Stargazing

Stories from Around the House

Kitchen, Bath Time, Bedtime

Before Storytime

Name Tags

Copy the name tags on pages 157–158. Make enough copies so you have one name tag per child; cut out and list each child's name. You may wish to pin each name tag on with a safety pin, copy the name tags onto removable adhesive paper, or punch a hole in the top of each name tag and string it with yarn for a necklace.

Props

- For your visit to the kitchen: wear an apron and a chef's hat. (I was able to get a paper one at a deli.) In your apron, place kitchen utensils in the pockets (a wooden spoon, spatula, rubber scraper, whisk, etc.).

- If you have difficulty finding a chef's hat, try a barbecue hat, or make one using white paper. Just create a white cardboard band to fit around your head and tape or staple white paper in a cylinder shape to the top.

- For your bath time stories, wear a shower cap on your head with a bathrobe. Place a towel over your shoulder and have some nice scented soap the children can smell. Can they guess what the scent is? You may also carry a bottle of bubble bath and even blow bubbles to attract the children's attention.

- For your bedtime stories wear pajamas and slippers, hold a blanket and teddy bear.

Storytime

- Introduce the theme by asking the children about their name tags.

- Show props and ask questions such as, "What room in the house do I look like I should be in?" "Do you know what these kitchen tools are used for?" "Have any of you used or seen these in your kitchen?" "What do you do before you go to bed?"

- Sing the storytime song on page 10.

- Intersperse stories, songs, fingerplays, and activities that fit within your time frame.

Snack

Kitchen Snack—Shaker Pudding

Supplies needed:

- instant pudding mix
- milk
- sealed container suitable for shaking

Directions:

1. Have the children help make pudding by placing instant pudding mix and milk in a well-sealed container.

2. Allow each child to take turns shaking. (Check by stirring with a spoon to make sure it is completely mixed before spooning out for all to enjoy.)

Bath Time Snack

Bubbly Fruit

Supplies needed:

- clear cups or glasses
- white soda
- fruit, such as strawberries, grapes, banana slices, blueberries, and pineapple.
- straws

Directions:

1. Place the fruit in the glass. Make it a learning experience and ask questions such as: "What colors are the fruits you have?" "Do you know what all the fruits are?" "Can you guess which ones will float and which ones will sink?"

2. Pour the white soda into the glass over the fruit. The children will need to use the straw to suck up many of the fruit pieces to be able to get them from the bottom. Show them that if they draw on the straw and hold their breath for just a moment, the straw will grab the fruit.

Bedtime Snack

- Serve good old-fashioned cookies and milk or hot chocolate.

Discussion Questions

Ask specific questions to reinforce compre-hension concepts, re-ignite excitement for the stories shared, enrich children's vocabu-lary, and influence narrative skills.

For example:

- "Would you want to take a bath if your bath time was like it was in the book *No Bath Tonight!*?"
- "Do you have anything in your house like in the book *There's a Wocket in My Pocket*?"
- "What was in Tom Farmer's kitchen?"
- "Who really made the mess in *Five Little Monkeys With Nothing to Do*?"
- "What snack did Lewis and the Beast have after his bath in *The Beast in the Bathtub*?"
- "Tell me some of the places the children decided to live in, in the story *Were Tired of Living in a House.*"

- "In the book, *Peace At Last*, where are some of the places Mr. Bear tries to sleep?" "Why is he still not able to sleep?"
- "Name some of the things the sheep counted to get to sleep in *Sheep Don't Count Sheep*?"

Wrapping It Up

Sing the song on page 11.

Songs

This Is the Way We Take a Bath

Author Unknown

Sung to the tune: "Mulberry Bush"

This is the way we take a bath,
Take a bath, take a bath.
This is the way we take a bath,
Splish! Splash! Splish!

This is the way we soap our toes ...

This is the way we wash our face ...

This is the way we wash our hair ...

(Continue with other body parts.)

This is the way we dry ourselves off,
Dry ourselves off, dry ourselves off.
This is the way we dry ourselves off,
All clean now!

Cleaning Song

Sung to the tune: "Row, Row, Row Your Boat"

Dust, dust, dust the chairs,
(Act as if you are dusting.)
Dust up high and low.
Cleaning can be fun,
If you sing as you go.

Mop, mop, mop the floors,
(Pretend to mop the floor.)
Mop them day or night.
When we wash we make them
Nice and white and bright.

Sweep, sweep, sweep the floor,
(Pretend to sweep the floor.)
Sweep them nice and clean.
Make the house all spic and span,
So we all stay healthy.

Clean Up Song

Author Unknown

Sung to the tune: "Frère Jacques"

Time to clean up.
Time to clean up.
Everybody help.
Everybody help.
Let's put all the toys away,
So we can play another day.
Thanks everyone!
Now let's go have more fun!

This is the Way

Variation of Traditional

Sung to the tune: "Mulberry Bush"

This is the way we clean the house,
(Pretend to dust and clean.)
Clean the house, clean the house.
This is the way we clean the house,
So early in the morning.

This is the way we sort the clothes,
*(Pretend to sort clothes, or have clothes to sort
during this part.)*
Sort the clothes, sort the clothes.
This is the way we sort the clothes,
So early in the morning.

This is the way we vacuum the house,
(Pretend to vacuum.)
Vacuum the house, vacuum the house.
This is the way we vacuum the house,
So early in the morning.

This is way we take a bath,
(Pantomime taking a bath.)
Take a bath, take a bath.
This is the way we take a bath,
After all our cleaning!

Take a Bath

Sung to the tune: "Row, Row, Row Your Boat"

Take, take, take a bath.
Take one every day.
Draw the water,
Get the toys,
And wash the germs away.

We All Clean Up

Sung to the tune: "Frère Jacques"

We all clean up,
We all clean up.

At my house,
At my house.

We all help in some way,
So we can have fun today.

We all help out,
And we don't pout.

Wash Your Hands

Author Unknown

Sung to the tune: "Row, Row, Row Your Boat"

Wash, wash, wash your hands.
Play our hand wash game.
Rub and scrub, and scrub and rub.
Germs go down the drain. Hey!

Wash, wash, wash your hands.
Play our hand wash game.
Rub and scrub, and scrub and rub.
Dirt goes down the drain. Hey!

Taking a Bath

Sung to the tune: "Skip to My Lou"

Take, take, take a bath,
(Pantomime taking a bath.)
Take, take, take a bath,
Take, take, take a bath,
Take one to get squeaky clean.

Play, play, play with your toys,
(Pantomime playing with toys in the tub.)
Play, play, play with your toys,
Play, play, play with your toys,
Splish and splash in the water.

Scrub, scrub, scrub in the tub,
(Pantomime scrubbing.)
Scrub, scrub, scrub in the tub,
Scrub, scrub, scrub in the tub,
Wash with soap and water.

Dry, dry, dry yourself off,
(Pantomime drying off.)
Dry, dry, dry yourself off,
Dry, dry, dry yourself off,
Now you're clean and snuggly! *(Hug self.)*

Soap-a-Float

Do as a rap, like "Pat-a-Cake."

Soap-a-float, soap-a-float, mommy and me.
Wash me as clean as I can be.
Scrub me and bathe me, and make me
squeaky clean.
Then towel me dry, and hug me happily!

Slippery Soap

Author Unknown

Do as a rap, like "Pat-a-Cake."

Slipp'ry, slipp'ry, slipp'ry soap.
(Pat thighs.)
Now you see it, now you don't!
Slide it on your arms 1–2–3.
(Match actions to words.)
Now your arms are slippery!

Slipp'ry, slipp'ry, slipp'ry soap. *(Pat thighs.)*
Now you see it, now you don't!
Slide it on your nose, 1–2–3.
(Match actions to words.)
Now your nose is slippery!

Continue with various other body parts.

Teddy Bear's Bath Time

Author Unknown

Do as a rap like with appropriate actions.

Teddy bear, teddy bear, climb in the tub
Teddy bear, teddy bear, scrub, scrub, scrub
Teddy bear, teddy bear, clean your toes
Teddy bear, teddy bear, wash your nose
Teddy bear, teddy bear, float your tug
Teddy bear, teddy bear, hop on the rug
Teddy bear, teddy bear, dry off so,
Teddy bear, teddy bear, to bed we go!

I Love Sheep

Author Unknown

Sung to the tune: "Three Blind Mice"

I love sheep, I love sheep.
I count them in my sleep.
They jump all night over fences high,
They jump so high they reach the sky.
They help me sleep, and this is why,
I love sheep, I love sheep.

Fingerplays

Pat-a-Cake

Traditional

Pat-a-cake, pat-a-cake, *(Clap hands together.)*
Baker's man,
Bake me a cake,
Just as fast as you can!

Roll it all around, *(Roll hand over hand.)*
And mark it with a "b,"
(Write a "b'" with your finger in the air.)
And put it in the oven for baby and me!
(Pretend to put a pan in the oven.)

Cleaning House (A face "fingerplay")

Author Unknown

First we open the windows.
(Close and open your eyes.)
Then we clean the blinds. *(Blink eyes.)*
Then we shake out the rugs.
(Stick out your tongue and shake it around.)
We clean the inside of the house.
(Rub tongue on the inside of one cheek, then the other side.)
Shake the broom out.
(Stick out your tongue and shake around.)
Open the door. *(Open your mouth.)*
And shut the gate.
(Close your teeth together, but leave your mouth open in a smile.)

Good Night

Author Unknown

Here is my room, *(Make box with hands.)*
And here is my bed. *(Spread hands out to side.)*
Here is the pillow, *(Put hands out in front.)*
For my sleepy head. *(Put hands under head.)*
Pull up the blankets, *(Pull hands up to neck.)*
Snuggle in tight. *(Wiggle.)*
Wait while I yawn, *(Yawn.)*
Then kiss me good night. *(Blow a big kiss.)*

Poems

I Don't Want to Go to Bed

"I don't want to go to bed," I said.
"I haven't even had my story read."
"We'll read it now," my dad said.
"Then you go to sleep, in your own bed."

Now it's quiet, I don't hear a peep.
Wait, it's Dad that's sound asleep! *(Snore!)*

Rub-a-Dub Dub

Traditional

Rub a dub dub,
Three men in a tub,
And who do you think they be?
The butcher, the baker,
The candlestick maker,
Give them a bath, all three!

There Is a Bed

Author Unknown

There is a bed inside my head.
And when the day is long,
I curl within my outside skin,
And sing myself a song.

Wee Willie Winkie

Traditional

Wee Willie Winkie runs through the town,
Upstairs, and downstairs, in his nightgown.
Rapping at the windows,
Crying through the lock,
"Are the children all in bed?
For it's now eight o'clock!"

Activities

Feather Duster Painting

After reading *There's a Wocket in My Pocket,* you might need to clean up. Show your feather duster and explain what its true use is for. Then paint with it!

Supplies needed:

- feathers (3 per duster)
- popsicle stick (1 per duster)
- masking tape
- paint
- paper
- dish soap

Directions:

1. Place three feathers together and tape to the end of a Popsicle stick to make a feather duster.

2. Use a plastic spoon to mix dish soap into your paint colors (this allows for easier clean-up, even with washable paint).

3. Allow the children to dip the feather duster into the paint and create their pictures on paper.

Bubble Art

After reading a bath time story, have the children make bubble pictures.

Supplies needed:

- soap bubbles
- food coloring
- paper
- paper towels
- dishes (amount needed depends on the number of colors you choose to have available)
- bubble wands

Directions:

1. Pour soap bubbles in individual dishes and add food coloring (make colors fairly dark).

2. Give the children a piece of paper and allow them to blow bubbles towards the paper. When the bubbles pop, they create a collage of color.

Tea in Bed: An Edible Art

Supplies needed:

- herbal fruit tea with honey
- cups for tea, 1 per child
- 1 slice of bread per child
- 2 regular marshmallows per child
- 1 graham cracker per child

Directions:

1. Give children a slice of bread, which represents the mattress, and have them spread out the sheets (spread with peanut butter). Place the pillow at the top of the bed (marshmallows), then put the blanket on top (graham cracker).

2. Serve with the tea that you have steeped in hot water.

Note: Steep the tea ahead of time and add the honey when warm. Serve either tepid or cold.

Gross Motor Activities

Clothesline Game

Sung to the tune: "Little Bunny Foo Foo"

I'm hanging up the wash,
The wash, the wash.
I'm hanging up the wash,
So all the clothes will dry.

Directions:

1. Have the children stand in a long line and pretend to hang clothes on the line as you sing the song above.

2. As they stand in the line, have them pretend the wind is blowing and ask them to move as the clothes would. Remind them they are the clothes on the line so they cannot move off the line. Only parts of their bodies are able to move. Have the wind blow softly, and then a bit harder.

Drying Game

Supplies needed:

- old bath towels or large dishcloths, 1 per child

Directions:

1. Give each child a towel.

2. Call out the names of body parts for the children to "dry off." For example, when you say "dry your elbow," the children place the towels on their elbows.

Bedtime!/Wake Up!

Directions:

1. Have the children stand so they can spread their arms out without touching their neighbor.

2. The children should listen for you to call out "bedtime" or "wake up."

3. When you call "bedtime," the children pretend to be asleep.

4. When you call "wake up," the children mime some things we do when we get up in the morning. Discuss ideas, such as get dressed, eat breakfast, stretch, etc.

Note: You may wish to set additional boundaries ahead of time, asking that the children do not move from the spot they are standing in now.

Math & Science Activity

Sink and Float

Supplies needed:

- sponge
- cork
- piece of paper
- rock
- bar of soap
- bolt or nut
- plastic tub with water
- plastic spoon
- ice cream scooper

Directions:

1. Show the children the above items and discuss what they are called and how they are used around the house.

2. Talk about what it means to sink or float.

3. Ask the children which items they think will sink or float.

4. Discuss which items are heavy and which are light. Which items are heavier than the water?

5. Place each item in the tub of water and see what happens.

6. Discuss the results, explaining the concept of heavy and light. Explain how items that were light became heavy by absorbing the water, thus making them heavier. Use the example of cereal in a bowl of milk. It may start out on top of the milk, but after time it will sink to the bottom of the bowl. The same thing has happened to the sponge.

Fine Motor Skills Activities

Kitchen Band

Supplies needed:

- plastic food containers with lids, such as empty ice cream buckets or sour cream, cottage cheese, or deli containers
- plastic spoons
- empty plastic water bottles with screw-top caps
- dried beans, peas, or rice
- aluminum pie plates (small disposable kind work best)
- duct tape

Directions:

1. Using a funnel, place beans, rice, or peas in the empty water bottles and screw the cap on tight. These make great shakers.

2. Place beans, rice, or peas in an aluminum pie plate and place another pie plate on top. Duct tape the edges together and make tambourines.

3. The empty plastic containers and plastic spoons can be the drums.

4. Hand out the "instruments" to the children, then put on some music or sing and enjoy the band! Rotate instruments if time allows.

    Note: You may wish to sing this song as the children play their instruments, adding conceptual skills such as fast, slow, loud, soft, etc.

    Sung to the tune: "Row, Row, Row Your Boat"

    Author Unknown

    Shake your shaker slowly,
    As slowly as can be.
    Shake your shaker slowly,
    Do it just like me.

    Shake your shaker quickly,
    As quickly as can be.
    Shake your shaker fast and quick,
    Do it just like me.

    Continue with the other instruments, taking turns helping all the children learn to follow directions, take turns, and be patient.

End with this song:

Sung to the tune: "Row, Row, Row Your Boat"

Let's all play now,
Play nice and loud.
Now let's play nice and soft,
And slowly all sit down.

Clothes Sort

Supplies needed:

- various types of clothes—socks, shirts, shorts, flip-flops, mittens, scarves, etc.

Directions:

1. Place the clothes out so the children can sort them by color.

2. Have them match similar items, like the socks that are the same or all the shirts.

3. Pair the items by the season they would be worn.

4. Discuss the concepts of seasons, enriching their vocabulary.

Storytime Books to Share

A Clean House for Mole and Mouse by Harriet Ziefert. Scholastic, 1988. Mole and Mouse clean house, but when Mole wants to do some other things Mouse has different ideas.

Cooking with the Cat by Bonnie Worth. Random House, 2003. Told with simple rhymes and rhythms, this jaunty illustrated tale gives very young readers a taste of the Cat in the Hat's flamboyant cooking skills as he slaps on a Chef's hat and whips up purple cupcakes using some truly odd ingredients!

Cows in the Kitchen by June Crebbin. Candlewick Press, 1988. While Tom Farmer is asleep under the haystack, the cows, ducks, pigs, hens, and sheep make quite a mess in the farmhouse.

Dancin' in the Kitchen by Wendy Gelsanliter and Frank Christian. Putnam, 1998. Dinnertime is dancing time at Grandma's house. While chicken and dumplings simmer on the stove, all three generations of the family have a hard time keeping still, grooving to the music on the kitchen radio. Their dancing creates some mighty big appetites, but will the merriment let up long enough for everyone to make it to the table?

The Feet in the Gym by Teri Daniels. Winslow Press, 1999. Handy Bob swings his mop and swabs the Lakeside gym with pride. This lovable school custodian is soon at his wit's end, however, as bustling students trek in dirt, grime, grit, and slime across his freshly mopped floor. Without missing a beat the children clear the mess with a wild and wonderful solution.

Five Little Monkeys with Nothing To Do by Eileen Christelow. Clarion Books, 2000. It's summer, school is out, and the five little monkeys are bored, so Mama suggests they clean the house for Aunt Bessie's visit. The five little monkeys clean their room and go on to sweep the floors, scrub the bathroom, and pick berries for dessert. But the results are deliciously messy!

Frog in the Kitchen Sink by Jim Post. Accord Publishing, 2001. Rhyming verse tells of the many places you shouldn't put a frog, such as your daddy's shoe, your granny's purse, and your sister's bed.

Gator Cleans House by Mercer Mayer. Green Frog, 1983. Gator is cleaning his house. But when his friends show up and try to help, they make the house messier than ever.

The House That Had Enough by P. E. King. Goldencraft, 1986. Tired of being mistreated, Anne's furniture, clothes, and house decide to leave until she promises to take better care of them.

How Do Dinosaurs Clean their Rooms? by Jane Yolen and Mark Teague. Blue Sky Press, 2004. See the various ways a dinosaur will tidy up his room.

Is this Maisy's House? by Lucy Cousins. Candlewick Press, 2004. Which house is Maisy's and which is her friend's? Lift the flaps and find out through picture clues.

Let's Clean Up! by Peggy Perry Anderson. Houghton Mifflin, 2002. A mother frog tackles the bedroom of her sloppy son, but before long, the little amphibian's room returns to ruin; his unorthodox attempts to clean it up himself bring humorous results.

The Man Who Didn't Wash His Dishes by Phyllis Krasilovsky. Doubleday, 1950. One night, a man who lives alone in a little house is just too tired to do his dishes after supper. So he decides to do them the next night ... until the same thing happens again, and again, until he has so many dirty dishes there is nowhere to sit in his house!

Max Cleans Up by Rosemary Wells. Viking, 2000. Max's big sister Ruby is determined to help him clean up his messy room, but he keeps rescuing things that she wants to throw away.

Mimi and the Dream House by Martin Waddell. Candlewick Press, 1998. Mimi wants to build Chez Mouse where, as she says, "I can be me!" First her sisters, then later her brothers, gather material and try to construct a dream home, each adding something to please themselves. Mimi doesn't like either of these abodes and finally builds one for herself.

A Mouse in the Marmalade by Jonathan Emmett. Tiger Tales, 2002. Cook has overslept and his kitchen has been overrun with all kinds of creatures. Lift the flaps in this rhyming story to find out who's hiding in the marmalade, the fruit bowl, and in surprising places all around the kitchen.

Mouse Mess by Linnea Riley. Blue Sky Press, 1997. A hungry mouse leaves a huge mess when it goes in search of a snack.

Mrs. McNosh Hangs Up Her Wash by Sarah Weeks. HarperTrophy, 1998. Mrs. McNosh hangs up her wash with such gusto that her clothesline ends up holding the dog, a Christmas wreath, a kite, and other odd items.

My World by Margaret Wise Brown. HarperCollins, 1949. A little bunny delights in all the familiar things in his daily life.

Oh, What a Mess by Hans Wilhelm. Crown Publishers, 1988. After Franklin Pig wins first prize in an art contest, his very messy family finally begins to put their dirty, messy home in order.

Paddington in the Kitchen by Michael Bond. HarperCollins, 1992. Paddington bakes a birthday cake. This board book, although small, has colorful pictures and a large enough font that will work with a smaller group of children.

Pots and Pans by Patricia Hubbell. HarperFestival, 1998. Rhyming text imitates Baby finding pots, pans, lids, and cans in the kitchen.

Robin's Room by Margaret Wise Brown. Hyperion, 2002. What do you do with a child who paints pictures on the doors and windows, plants flowers in the bathtub, and hides his toys under the rug? Why, you give him a room of his own, of course!

The Someday House by Anne Shelby. Orchard Books, 1996. Describes what it would be like to live in a house on a mountain, by the sea, above the bakery, underground, and in other wonderful places.

Spot Bakes a Cake by Eric Hill. Putnam, 1994. Spot helps his mother make his father's birthday cake.

Super-Completely and Totally the Messiest by Judith Viorst. Atheneum, 2001. Olivia, who is very neat and practically perfect, despairs because her sister Sophie is super-completely and totally the messiest person, no matter where she goes or what she does.

There's a Wocket In My Pocket! by Dr. Seuss. Random House, 1974. Silly rhyming words describe many items in a house.

This Mess by Pam Conrad. Hyperion, 1998. While Daddy makes spaghetti sauce in the kitchen, Elizabeth, Sophia, and Salvatore clean up the mess in the living room and give it a fantastic appearance.

Warthogs in the Kitchen: A Sloppy Counting Book by Pamela Duncan Edwards. Hyperion, 1998. Three warthogs count to ten as they bake cupcakes.

We Were Tired of Living in a House by Liesel Moak Skorpen. Putnam, 1999. Four children move to a tree, a raft, a cave, and finally the seashore, enjoying each new dwelling until they discover its drawbacks.

When Young Melissa Sweeps by Nancy Byrd Turner. Peachtree Publishers, 1998. Describes how a young girl curtsies and whirls, and waltzes and jigs as she sweeps the house.

Bath Time Stories

Bath Time by Eileen Spinelli. Marshall Cavendish, 2003. A child fills up his bathtub with so many toys that there is no room for him in it.

The Beast in the Bathtub by Kathleen Stevens. Gareth Stevens, 1985. Lewis gets into mischief with an imaginary beast in the bathtub while his parents are watching television.

Bernard's Bath by Joan Elizabeth Goodman. Boyd's Mills Press, 1996. When a little elephant refuses to take a bath, his parents must show him how much fun bath time can be.

Bubbles, Bubbles by Kathi Appelt. HarperFestival, 2001. In this exuberant book, an appealing, dirty-faced, grime-covered toddler has a bath and a shampoo. The rhymed text ("Bubbles, bubbles in the tubbles, / splishy, splashy, splooshy scrubbles") makes good use of sounds that describe the process of getting clean.

Dad's Car Wash by Harry Sutherland. Atheneum, 1988. John's love of cars and trucks follows him to the bathtub, where he drives himself into Dad's Car Wash and gets the works.

Dirty Little Boy by Margaret Wise Brown. Winslow Press, 2001. When a little boy tries to get clean the way different animals do, he only gets dirtier.

Just Me in the Tub by Mercer Mayer. Golden Books, 1994. Little Critter takes a bath.

Little Bunny's Bathtime! by Jane Johnson. Tiger Tales, 2004. It's time for Mrs. Rabbit to give her children a bath, but her youngest Little Bunny would rather keep on playing, and he'll do anything to get her attention.

Max's Bath by Rosemary Wells. Dial, 1998. Ruby gives her brother Max two baths, but he winds up dirtier than ever.

Mother Makes a Mistake by Ann Dorer. Gareth Stevens, 1991. Knowing Kate would rather play than bathe, Mother mistakes the word for bath, substituting other words so many times, Kate finally insists on being given a bath.

No Bath Tonight! by Harriet Ziefert. DK Publishing, 1997. It's bath time, but the little boy would much rather think of good reasons not to get in the tub.

No More Water in the Tub! by Tedd Arnold. Puffin, 1998. William is getting ready for his bath when the faucet breaks, sending him and his tub surfing through the building! On his wet ride, he collects a strange fleet in his wake—from Uncle Nash, who sits in the trash, to Little Dottie, who sails the potty.

Scrubba Dub by Nancy Van Laan. Atheneum, 2003. Mamma bunny tries to bathe her energetic toddler.

Splish, Splash! by Sarah Weeks. Harper Trophy, 2000. Rub-a-dub-dub! Chub the fish loves to scrub in his tub. One day his friends come to call. They want to splish and splash too. Can a tub so small hold them all?

Tub Toys by Terry Miller Shannon and Timothy Warner. Tricycle Press, 2002. With playful pictures and funny rhymes, this book proves that kids can never have too many bath toys—or can they?

Bedtime Stories

All the Way to Morning by Marc Harshman. Marshall Cavendish, 1999. All around the world, different children hear different sounds as they get ready to sleep.

A Bedtime Story by Mem Fox. Mondo Publishing, 1996. Polly and her friend Bed Rabbit have lots of books, but they don't know how to read, so Polly's parents interrupt their own reading for a bedtime story.

Bedtime Story by Rose Greydanus. Troll, 1988. When his children claim they are not sleepy at bedtime, father finds an entertaining way to get them to bed.

Can't Sleep by Kees Moerbeek. Price Stern Sloan, 1994. A pop-up book featuring jungle animals that cannot sleep because someone is watching them.

Can't You Sleep, Little Bear? by Martin Waddell. Candlewick Press, 1992. When bedtime comes, Little Bear is afraid of the dark, until Big Bear brings him lights and love.

The Dreamtime Fairies by Jane Simmons. Little, Brown and Company, 2002. Lucy, Bear, Jamie, and Floppy Rabbit fly across the ocean to find the Dreamtime Fairies who will help them fall asleep.

Fred's Bed by Marilyn Singer. HarperFestival, 2001. Fred needs a new bed and his mother has some suggestions, but Fred does not like any until she suggests a big soft mattress.

Good Night, Gorilla by Peggy Rathmann. Putnam, 1994. The zookeeper thinks it's the same old bedtime routine, but all bets are off when a furry little ape gets hold of the keys. One by one Gorilla lets the other animals out, until a silent, silly lion follows the zookeeper home. The end of the story for the zookeeper is just the beginning for his put-upon spouse, however.

Goodnight Moon by Margaret Wise Brown. HarperCollins, 1947. In a great green room, tucked away in bed, is a little bunny. "Goodnight room, goodnight moon." And to all the familiar things in the softly lit room—to the picture of the three little bears sitting in chairs, to the clocks and his socks, to the mittens and the kittens, to everything one by one—he says goodnight.

Hide and Sleep by Melanie Walsh. DK Publishing, 1999. At bedtime, Princess Poppy decides that, instead of going to bed, she is going to hide, trying several hiding places before the perfect one.

How Do Dinosaurs Say Goodnight? by Jane Yolen. Blue Sky Press, 2000. Mother and child ponder the different ways a dinosaur can say goodnight, from slamming his tail and pouting to giving a big hug and kiss.

How to Make a Night by Linda Ashman. HarperCollins, 2004. After a hectic day, it is time to bring on the night so that a child and her family can finally rest.

I Hate to Go to Bed! by Katie Davis. Harcourt Brace, 1999. Convinced that her parents are having a party after she goes to bed, a little girl devises several plans to find out what's she missing.

Lullabyhullaballoo! by Mick Inkpen. Hodder Children's Books, 1993. A princess has trouble getting to sleep, until some clanking knights, snorting dragons, eerie ghosts, and forest creatures come to her aid.

The Monster Under My Bed by Suzanne Gruber. Troll, 1985. At bedtime, a little bear finds that there is a logical explanation for those monster noises coming from beneath his bed.

The Napping House by Audrey Wood. Harcourt, 1984. In this cumulative tale, a wakeful flea atop a number of sleeping creatures causes a commotion, with just one bite.

Nighty Night! by Margaret Wild and Kerry Argent. Peachtree Publishers, 2000. Little lambs, chicks, ducks, and pigs change places and try other ways to delay going to bed.

Peace At Last by Jill Murphy. Dial, 1980. Mr. Bear tries to sleep, but everywhere he goes noises keep him up.

Sheep Don't Count Sheep by Margaret Wise Brown. Margaret K. McElderry Books, 2003. A little lamb has trouble falling asleep, until his mother tells him to count the butterflies that flutter past his closed eyes.

So Many Bunnies: A Bedtime ABC and Counting Book by Rick Walton and Paige Miglio. HarperCollins, 1998. Old Mother Rabbit's 26 children, each named for a letter of the alphabet, are lovingly put to bed.

Ten in the Bed by Penny Dale. Walker & Co., 1990. A little boy and all his stuffed animals fit into a bed, until they start falling out.

The Very Noisy Night by Diana Hendry. Dutton Children's Books, 1999. Little Mouse is frightened by all the different sounds he hears at bedtime, but Big Mouse always knows just what that sound is.

What Was That! by Geda Bradley Mathews. Goldencraft, 1975. Three skittish brothers try to comfort each other when they hear night noises in their house.

When Sheep Cannot Sleep: The Counting Book by Satoshi Kitamura. Farrar, Straus and Giroux, 1988. When Wooly the sheep suffers from insomnia, he goes for a walk and gets into just about everything. Each illustration features objects for children to count.

Name Tag Patterns for Stories from Around the House

Name Tag Patterns for Stories from Around the House

The Great Outdoors
Camping, Fishing, Canoeing, Hiking, Wildlife

Before Storytime

Name Tags

Copy the name tags on pages 170–172. Make enough copies so you have one name tag per child; cut out and list each child's name. You may wish to pin each name tag on with a safety pin, copy the name tags onto removable adhesive paper, or punch a hole in the top of each name tag and string it with yarn for a necklace.

Props

Wear comfortable, casual clothes, a hat, hiking boots, and a backpack. Place a pair of binoculars and/or a camera around your neck. Hold a fishing pole (without the hook) or walking stick. If you have access to a canoe or kayak paddle, also bring that to show.

Storytime

- Introduce the theme by asking the children about their name tags.

- Place woodland puppets in your backpack. This will aid in drawing attention at storytime. You may wish to have one of the puppets stick out of the backpack and pretend you don't know it is there. As you walk around you could mention you feel something tickling your back; what could it be? Pretend to be shocked by the animal in your backpack. You can use this as a springboard for discussion on animal safety in the woods.

- Sing the storytime song on page 10.

- Intersperse stories, songs, fingerplays, and activities that fit within your time frame.

Snack

- Serve apple juice with a healthy trail mix. Use various nuts, dried fruit, and dried berries. Have the children help pour, add, and mix everything together. Introduce what nuts, fruits, and berries you have to blend. Discuss the differences in appearance of the fruit and nuts before and after they are dried. Also, talk about where the nuts come from, e.g., pumpkin seeds, sunflower seeds, etc.

- A great "take-along" snack is to place trail mix in a plastic bag.

Discussion Questions

Ask specific questions to reinforce comprehension concepts, re-ignite excitement for the stories shared, enrich children's vocabulary, and influence narrative skills.

For example:

- "What are some of the animals that came into the canoe in *One-Dog Canoe?*"

- "Who sleeps with the girl in the book *My Camp-Out?*" "Where does she camp out?"

- "What does Little Loon finally learn how to do in *Little Loon and Papa?*"

- "Where did Turtle and Snake end up roasting marshmallows in *Turtle and Snake Go Camping?*" "Why did they end up there?"

- "What was Rebecca building when she saw the moose in the book *Even that Moose Won't Listen To Me?*"

- Utilize the back pages of *When We Go Camping* and have the children discuss the animals listed and "I Spy" them. Discuss what other things they see in the paintings. Discuss the difference between what other books have for illustrations, and that these are paintings, not drawings. Talk about those that have gone camping and where they have been. Ask, "Have they seen moose like in the book when they've gone camping?"

Wrapping It Up

Sing the song on page 11.

Songs

A Camping We Will Go

Author Unknown

Sung to the tune: "The Farmer in the Dell"

Do appropriate actions.

A camping we will go,
A camping we will go.
Hi ho, we're off to the woods,
A camping we will go.

Oh, don't forget the tent,
No, don't forget the tent.
Hi ho, we're off to the woods,
A camping we will go.

We'll have to pack some food,
We'll have to pack some food.
Hi ho, we're off to the woods,
A camping we will go.

We'll have to collect some wood,
We'll have to collect some wood.
Hi ho, we're off to the woods,
A camping we will go.

Now let's make the fire,
Now let's make the fire.
Be careful now don't get too close,
To our big camp fire.

It's time to pitch the tent,
It's time to pitch the tent.
Hi ho, we're in the woods,
Look at us camping now!

When I Go Camping

Sung to the tune: "Skip To My Lou"

When I go camping I bring a tent,
When I go camping I bring a tent,
When I go camping I bring a tent,
And a sleeping bag.

Additional verses: book, flashlight, pillow, etc.

Ask the children what they would bring and use that as a verse.

I'm Going Camping

Author Unknown

Sung to the tune: "Twinkle, Twinkle, Little Star"

I'm going camping, yessireee!
I'm going camping, won't you come with me?

First we'll pitch our tent on the ground.
Then we'll make a fire and gather 'round.

I'm going camping, yessireee!
I'm going camping, won't you come with me?

Next we'll cook on the open fire,
Then we'll tell stories till we all get tired.
When the stars are twinkling bright,
We'll sleep in our tents till the morning light.

I'm going camping, yessireee!
I'm going camping, won't you come with me?

When we see the morning sun,
We'll wake right up 'cause the day's begun!
There's so much that we can do,
Fishing, swimming, hiking, too.

I'm going camping, yessireee!
I'm going camping, won't you come with me?

Directional Song

Author Unknown

Sung to the tune: "Row, Row, Row Your Boat"

North, South, East, or West,
Which way do I go?
If only I had a compass,
Then I'd surely know!

Raccoon

Author Unknown

Sung to the tune: "Kookaburra"

Raccoon sleeps in a hollow tree,
While the sun shines on you and me.
Sleep raccoon, sleep raccoon,
Warm and cozily.

In the darkest part of night,
Raccoon has the best eyesight.
Look raccoon, look raccoon,
My, your eyes are bright!

Raccoon hardly makes a sound,
When he prowls around.
Hunt raccoon, hunt raccoon,
Find food on the ground.

Along the Trail

Author Unknown

Sung to the tune: "Frère Jacques"

Let's go hiking, let's go hiking, *(Beckon with hand.)*
Along the trail, along the trail.
I love to hike fast, *(Mimic action.)*
I love to hike slow, *(Mimic action.)*
Along the trail, along the trail.

Substitute other actions for hike, such as climb and walk (mimic actions).

Do Your Antlers Hang High?

Author Unknown

Sung to the tune: "Do Your Ears Hang Low?"

Do your antlers hang high?
Do they reach up to the sky?
Do they keep you up at night?
Do they make your way so tight?
Do they bump into trees?
Do they make it hard for knees?
Do your antlers hang high?

Over the River

Author Unknown

Sung to the tune: "Over the River"

Over the river, along the trail,
The hikers march along.
And as they go, they love to sing,
Their favorite hiking song.

Over the river, along the trail,
They love to hike and sing.
They're filled with all the wonders,
A nature hike can bring.

Owl

Author Unknown

Sung to the tune: "I'm a Little Teapot"

Owl in the treetop,
(Place hands around eyes; spread arms out and up for a tree.)

Proud and wise.
(Hands under armpits; stick out chest, then point to head.)
Here are his wings,
(Hands under armpits; flap.)
And here are his eyes. *(Point to eyes.)*
Down on the ground, *(Point to ground.)*
A mouse he spies.
(Move fingers quickly facing the ground.)
Up he jumps, *(Fly hands up.)*
And off he flies! *(Flap wings.)*

Fingerplays

Hiss Goes the Snake

Hiss, hiss, hiss, said the snake to me.
(Hiss and point to self.)
Hiss, hiss, hiss, he looks like an "S," can you see? *(Draw an "s" in the air.)*
Hiss, hiss, hiss, he slithers away.
(Use hand or arm to mimic a snake slithering.)
Maybe we'll see him again on another day.
(Place hand over eyes as if viewing far away.)

Five Frisky Frogs

Author Unknown

Five frisky frogs,
Hopping on the shore,
One hopped into the pond—SPLASH!
So now there are four.

Four frisky frogs,
Climbing up a tree.
One fell into the grass—OUCH!
So now there are three.

Three frisky frogs,
Bathing in the dew,
One caught a cold and sneezed—ACHOO!
Now there are two.

Two frisky frogs,
Sleeping in the sun,
One slept the day away—SNORE!
So now there is just one.

One frisky frog,
Sitting on a stone.
Let's call his four friends back—YOO-HOO!
So he won't be alone.

This is My Turtle

Author Unknown

This is my turtle,
(Make a fist and extend thumb.)
He lives in a shell. *(Hide thumb in fist.)*
He likes his home very well.
He pokes his head out when he wants to eat,
(Extend thumb.)
And pulls it back in when he wants to sleep.
(Hide thumb in fist.)

The Biggest Tree of All

Author Unknown

See me growing up so tall.
(Hold fists close together.)
I'm the biggest tree of all.
(Slowly open fists with fingers spread up.)
My branches hold the biggest nests.
(Make a circle with both hands.)
The big birds tweet a big "goodbye."
(Wave goodbye.)
And flap their wings—away they fly!
(Join thumbs together; flap fingers.)

Ricky Raccoon

Author Unknown

Ricky Raccoon is a bandit they say,
(Place fingers and thumbs over eyes.)
He'll steal your vittles and scurry away.
(Mime grabbing things; run with fingers.)
So if you go camping, watch out for this guy,
(Place fingers and thumbs over eyes.)
He'll snatch up your lunch in the wink of an
eye! *(Wink.)*

The Turtle

Author Unknown

There was a little turtle who lived in a box.
(Place hand over fist.)
He swam in the puddles and climbed on
the rocks. *(Wiggle fingers; climb fingers on other
hand's closed fist.)*
He snapped at a mosquito, *(Snap fingers.)*
He snapped at a flea, *(Snap fingers.)*
He snapped at a minnow, *(Snap fingers.)*
And he snapped at me! *(Snap fingers together;
point to self.)*

He caught the mosquito, *(Make grabbing
motion with fingers in the air.)*

He caught the flea, *(Make grabbing motion with
fingers in the air.)*
He caught the minnow, *(Make grabbing motion
with fingers in the air.)*
But he didn't catch me! *(Point to self; shake
head.)*

Bullfrog

Author Unknown

Here is Mr. Bullfrog,
(Left hand closed, thumb upright.)
Sitting on a rock.
Along comes a little boy,
(Walking motion with index and third finger.)
And Mr. Bullfrog jumps—KERPLOP!
(Thumb makes diving motion.)

Going Fishing

Author Unknown

When I go fishing down at the brook,
(Pretend to hold a fishing pole over your shoulder.)
I put a wiggly worm on my hook.
(Pretend to put a worm on a hook.)
I toss it in the water and hope with all my
might, *(Swing line in water.)*
A little fish will swim by, *(Place hand on side,
thumb up, fingers together, and wiggle.)*
And take a big bite.
*(With other hand, move thumb and forefinger
together in a snapping motion while moving oppo-
site hand like a fish.)*

Mr. Moose

Author Unknown

Mr. Moose is very tall,
(Raise arms above head; stand tall.)
His antlers touch the sky.
(Reach hands out and spread arms wide.)
They make a real good resting place,
For birdies passing by.
(Lock thumbs and flap fingers like a bird's wings.)

One Fine Day

Author Unknown

One fine day in the woods I saw, *(Place hand
over eyes as if looking far away.)*
A bear in a honey tree, licking his paw.
(Pretend to lick paw.)
A bee buzzed by, and what do you suppose?
(Wave forefinger and buzz.)

The bee stung the bear on the tip of his nose! *(Point to nose.)*
"Ouch!" said the bear as he slid down the tree, *(Pretend to slide down a tree.)*
"I do like honey, but I don't like the bees!" *(Rub tummy; shake finger back and forth.)*

My Turtle

Author Unknown

My turtle has a shell, *(Point index finger; cover all but the tip of it with the other hand.)*
He walks from side to side. *(Wiggle finger of first hand as you move sideways.)*
I guess it is a mobile home, *(Move hand back and forth.)*
Where he can go and hide. *(Quickly pull in index finger.)*

Five Little Bears

Author Unknown

Five little bears were sitting on the ground. *(Hold up five fingers.)*

Five little bears made a deep growling sound—GRRRR!

The first one said, "Let's have a look around." *(Hold up first finger.)*

The second one said, "I feel rather funny." *(Hold up two fingers.)*

The third one said, "I think I smell honey!" *(Hold up three fingers.)*

The fourth one said, "Shall we climb up the tree?" *(Hold up four fingers.)*

The fifth one said, "Look out! There's a bee!" *(Hold up five fingers.)*

So five little bears went back to their play. *(Hide hand.)*

And decided to wait until the bees flew away. *(Use first finger to mimic a bee flying.)*

Poems

Bear Fishing

Author Unknown

When a bear goes fishing in the cool brook,
He doesn't have a pole or a worm on a hook.

When he sees a fish go by, as quick as can be,
He snatches up a meal for himself,
And he doesn't share with me!

His paws are all he uses,
when he wants a fish to eat.
It seems his way of fishing,
really can't be beat!

Moose Pride

Author Unknown

If I were a moose,
I'd be proud of my nose.
As big as a house,
And as long as a hose.
I'd smell every raindrop,
Or pine tree, or rose.
I would be so happy,
I'd dance on my toes.

If I were a moose,
I'd be proud to stand tall.
I'd walk through deep rivers,
No problem at all.
My legs could step over
Dead trees where they fall.
I'd see all around me
Because I'd be so tall.

If I were a moose,
I'd be proud of my head,
With antlers that spread out
As wide as a shed.
A perch for the birdies,
Brown, yellow, and red.
I'd be proud of the antlers,
On top of my head.

Activities

Nature Painting

Supplies needed:

- leaves
- gummy worms
- rocks
- sticks
- paint
- toothbrushes
- watercolors
- dandelions (yellow)

- paper
- flowers
- feathers
- old shirts to cover clothes

Directions:

1. Create reverse paintings by placing anything from nature that will lay flat down on a piece of paper. Arrange the items in a pattern. Use multiple items for a whole picture effect.

2. Dip the toothbrushes in paint and run your thumb over the bristles that are facing downward towards the paper, to splatter the paint around the object.

3. Lift your object off the paper for your "reverse print."

4. You may also use the dandelions to paint with on white paper. If rubbed fairly hard, they will "paint" by staining the paper.

5. Paint with the gummy worms as well as using them for the reverse painting—just make sure you have extras to eat!

Camping Lanterns

Supplies needed:

- toilet paper tube
- yellow construction paper
- small piece of yarn
- orange cellophane
- cardboard
- hole punch
- scissors
- glue

Directions:

1. Cut a small circle out of cardboard approximately 3" in diameter.

2. Using the hole punch, punch designs in the toilet paper tube. Punching in clusters can create various patterns such as stars or flower-like shapes.

3. To create a "door" in the toilet paper tube, cut up from the bottom of the tube about 2¾" and across about 2".

4. Glue the tube onto the center of the circle.

5. Cut a piece of construction paper about 2" x 2". Roll into a tube and glue the sides to form the candlestick.

6. Add a piece of orange cellophane by twisting the end and fitting it into the top of the candlestick.

7. Punch a hole on either side of the top of the toilet paper tube and string yarn through, making your lantern handle. Knot the yarn until it can no longer go through your holes.

Marshmallow People

Supplies needed:

- toothpicks
- marshmallows
- food coloring

Directions:

1. Use toothpicks and marshmallows to create a person.

2. Dip a toothpick in the food coloring to add a mouth and eyes.

Hiking Water Bottles

Supplies needed:

- plastic water bottles with caps (1 per child)
- orange bags (the plastic weaved kind)
- yarn
- scissors
- stickers

Directions:

1. Let the children place stickers on the outsides of the water bottles.

2. Place the water bottle in the orange bag and trim the bag down so it is approximately 2" longer than the water bottle.

3. Cut two pieces of yarn long enough to go over the child's shoulder with approximately 2" to spare.

4. Fish one end of each piece of yarn through the netting (it helps if you tape the end of the yarn), one at a time,

but next to each other. This will give it strength.

5. Tie a knot in the end on the inside of the bag. Repeat.

6. They now have a handy carrier for their water bottles as they hike!

   Note: An option for older children would be to give them each three pieces of yarn (the same length), and demonstrate braiding. Have them braid their yarn before tying it onto the bag, making it stronger.

Who's Sleeping in the Tent?

Supplies needed:

- blue and green construction paper
- scissors
- glue
- markers/crayons
- old magazines

Directions:

1. Cut a large triangle out of the blue construction paper approximately 9" across at the base.

2. Cut a slit about 3½" up from the bottom on an angle to represent the tent flap.

3. Have the children glue the triangle onto the green construction paper. Glue only the corners of the triangle so the flap can open.

4. Have them to color the paper and add whatever they want to their campsite picture.

5. Have the children cut out pictures from the magazines, or have pre-cut pictures ready for the children to glue under the flap as a surprise—"who is sleeping in my tent?"—aspect to their picture.

Gross Motor Activity

Scavenger Hunts

Supplies needed:

- paper lunch bags (1 per child)
- index cards

- small squares of construction paper in various colors found in nature
- basic shapes cut from the same colors of construction paper
- small squares of wallpaper in various textures
- small squares of craft foam
- small squares of plastic wrap or cellophane
- marker or pen
- pictures/glue (*optional*)

Directions:

1. Cut several squares of the above listed items.

2. Cut out the shapes from the construction paper (one of each shape is all that is needed).

3. On index cards, write a word for an item you wish the children to find and draw a picture next to the word on the card or glue a picture next to the word.

4. Place the various squares in a bag and shake it to mix them up.

5. Give the children their lunch bags.

6. Have each child pick one square out of the bag.

7. If they pick a construction paper square, have them find something on the ground that matches that color.

8. If they choose one of the other squares, discuss the texture and ask them to find something on the ground that matches that texture. Is it spongy or rubbery? Is it smooth or rough? This is a great way to use expanded vocabulary with the children, to not only teach concepts, but also pre-reading skills.

9. If a child chooses a shape, ask them to "I Spy" that shape within nature. It does not have to be something they can pick up. It could be a crook in a tree the shape of a puddle, etc.

   Note: If the weather does not permit this to be an outside activity, you can move it indoors by "planting" items around the room.

Math & Science Activity

The Force of Nature

Supplies needed:

- various items from outdoors, such as rocks, feathers, pinecones of various shapes and sizes, etc.
- kitchen scale
- paper
- marker

Directions:

1. Lay out the various items you collected from outside. You might want to collect the items with the children on a nature walk.

2. Write the word "heavy" on one piece of paper and "light" on another. Have the children say the letter names as you write them.

3. Ask the children to predict which items they think will be heavy and which they think will be light by placing them on the appropriate paper.

4. Count the number of items the children have placed on each paper. Write that number on the paper.

5. Weigh the items and count how many are light, as well as how many are heavy.

6. You may even wish to write down how much each item weighed.

7. Discuss how even though some items are the same size (pinecones, rocks, etc.) they do not weigh exactly the same.

8. You could also chart how many items the children guessed correctly (heavy or light).

   Note: A variation of this could be a sink and float test with the same items, using a bowl of water.

Fine Motor Skills Activity

Nature Sort/What's Missing Game

Supplies needed:

- pinecones
- rocks/stones
- feathers
- seed pods
- leaves

Directions:

1. Collect multiples of the above items, making sure you take only from the ground (so as not to harm nature).

2. Before placing items out to sort, place some of them in a backpack.

3. Bring one item out at a time. For children of this age, it is best to show no more than a few items at a time. Discuss what the item is, where it came from, and its purpose in nature.

4. Place all the items back in the backpack, and bring out all but one item from the bag. Ask the children, "What's missing?"

5. After this game, place all the items on a table and have the children sort according to classification. You may suggest categories such as texture, where it came from, the letter it begins with, or color.

Storytime Books to Share

ABCs Naturally: A Child's Guide to the Alphabet through Nature by Lynne Smith Diebel and Jann Faust Kalscheur. Trails Books, 2003. Each letter of the alphabet features an object photographed in nature accompanied by a short poem.

Antler, Bear, Canoe, a Northwoods Alphabet Year by Betsy Bowen. Houghton Mifflin, 1991. Introduces the letters of the alphabet in woodcut illustrations and brief text depicting the changing seasons in the northern woods.

Antlers Forever! by Frances Bloxam. Down East Books, 2001. Orville, the moose, is a likable young fellow who tries very hard to do everything right, especially when it comes to taking care of his handsome pair of antlers. But despite all his care, he wakes up one day to find that they are coming loose!

Backyard Bedtime by Susan Hill. Harper Growing Tree, 2001. Say goodnight to all of nature as children get ready for bed.

A Camping Spree with Mr. Magee by Chris Van Dusen. Chronicle Books, 2003. Mr. Magee and his dog Dee go camping and have an adventure with a hungry bear.

Coyote Raid in Cactus Canyon by Jim Arnosky. Putnam, 2005. Four young coyotes harass the animals in the desert canyon until they run into a rattlesnake.

Down By the Cool of the Pool by Tony Mitton. Orchard Books, 2002. Frog and the other animals have a dancing good time both in and out of the water in the cool of the pool.

Down in the Woods at Sleepytime by Carole Lexa Schaefer. Candlewick Press, 2000. When their mothers announce that it is bedtime, the baby animals of the forest express their objections, but when wise Grandma Owl hoots that it's storytime, they respond differently.

Even that Moose Won't Listen to Me by Martha Alexander. Dial, 1988. A little girl tries various means to get rid of a giant moose in the garden after she repeatedly warns her family and they refuse to believe her.

Frog Hunt by Sandra Jordan. Roaring Brook Press, 2002. A group of children set out on a summer morning to catch a frog, and along the way they observe a muskrat, minnows, and a fish as well.

Give Her the River: A Father's Wish for His Daughter by Michael Dennis Browne. Atheneum, 2004. A father dreams of all the things he will give his young daughter.

The Giving Tree by Shel Silverstein. Harper & Row, 1964. This story of a boy who grows to manhood, and of a tree that gives him her bounty through the years, is a moving parable about the gift of giving and the capacity to love.

Good Morning, Pond by Alyssa Satin Capucilli. Hyperion, 1994. The leap of a little green frog signals the start of a new day as the creatures of the pond awake and go through a variety of morning rituals.

Gordon Goes Camping by Julie Brinckloe. Doubleday, 1975. When he is finally ready to go camping, Gordon adds one more thing to his supplies—a friend to help him carry them.

Hello Muddah, Hello Faddah! (A Letter From Camp) by Allan Sherman and Lou Busch. Dutton Children's Books, 2004. Funny and bright illustrations add to the fun of this book, based on the song of the same name.

If You Give a Moose a Muffin by Laura Joffe Numeroff. HarperCollins, 1991. Chaos can ensue if you give a moose a muffin and start him on a cycle of urgent requests.

In the Small, Small Pond by Denise Fleming. Henry Holt & Company, 1993. Gives young readers a frog's-eye view of life in a pond throughout the seasons. A Caldecott Honor book.

In the Tall, Tall Grass by Denise Fleming. Henry Holt & Company, 1991. Rhymed text presents a toddler's view of creatures found in the grass from lunchtime till nightfall, such as bees, ants, and moles.

In the Woods: Who's Been Here? by Lindsay Barrett George. Greenwillow Books, 1995. Come follow the trail with a boy and a girl as clue after clue tells them what bird or animal has been there.

I Went to the Bay by Ruth Miller. Kids Can Press, 1999. A boy goes in search of frogs. To his surprise, he discovers a vibrant, bustling world of wildlife in and around a bay, where a hummingbird hovers over a flower, a turtle buries itself in the sand and a bullfrog goes "harump." The bay provides a day's fascination for the curious little boy—and a day's fun for some elusive frogs.

Jump, Frog, Jump! by Robert Kalan. Greenwillow Books, 1981. When a frog catches a fly, he sets off a chain of predators.

Just Fishing With Grandma by Gina and Mercer Mayer. Golden Books, 2003. Little Critter wants to go fishing, but everyone is busy until Grandma volunteers.

Little Bear's Little Boat by Eve Bunting. Clarion Books, 2003. When Little Bear can no longer fit into his boat, he finds someone else who can use it.

Little Loon and Papa by Toni Buzzeo. Dial, 2004. Motivated by a challenging situation and his supportive father, Little Loon finally learns to dive.

Loon Lake by Jonathan London. Chronicle Books, 2002. A girl and her father encounter loons and other lake creatures during a magical nighttime canoe ride.

Lost in the Woods: A Photographic Fantasy by Carl Sams. Carl Sams II Photography, Inc., 2004. A spring tale of trust and patience. Woodland creatures are concerned for a newborn white-tailed fawn they believe is lost.

Lost Moose by Jan Slepian. Philomel Books, 1995. A moose calf separated from his mother encounters a boy who follows him on a long walk through the woods, until they are both reclaimed by their respective mothers.

Maisy Goes Camping by Lucy Cousins. Candlewick Press, 2004. Maisy and her friends go camping, with interesting results.

Mooses Come Walking by Arlo Guthrie. Chronicle Books, 1995. Describes the activities of moose as they walk and wander, and even look in the window at you lying in bed.

Moose in the Garden by Nancy Carlstrom. Harper & Row, 1990. A young child is delighted when Papa Moose visits the garden and eats almost all the vegetables.

Mr. Bear's Vacation by Debi Gliori. Orchard Books, 2000. When Mr. Bear's relaxing camping trip with his family turns into a scary nightmare, he decides they need a vacation from their vacation.

Mucky Moose by Jonathan Allen. Macmillan, 1990. Mucky, the muckiest, smelliest moose in the forest, proves that smelling bad has its advantages when trying to outwit a fierce wolf.

My Camp-Out by Marcia Leonard. Millbrook Press, 1999. A young girl camps out in her bedroom and is joined by her mother. Real photographs illustrate this story.

Nature Walk by Douglas Florian. Greenwillow Books, 1989. Two children walk through the woods with a guide, exploring trails and observing nature around them.

Not Just Another Moose by Stephanie Greene. Marshall Cavendish, 2000. When Moose's magnificent antlers fall off, he discovers he has other remarkable features as well.

Once There Was a Tree by N. Romanova. Puffin, 1989. An old stump attracts many living creatures, even man, and when it is gone, a new tree attracts the same creatures, which need it for a variety of reasons.

One-Dog Canoe by Mary Casanova. Farrar, Straus and Giroux, 2003. A girl and her dog set out in their canoe one morning, only to be insistently joined by a series of animals, large and small.

P. J. Funnybunny Camps Out by Marilyn Sadler. Random House, 1993. Although P. J. and his friends refuse to let Donna and Honey Bunny go camping with them because "camping is not for girls," the girls follow and get proof that camping is hard work even for boys.

Quiet Night by Marilyn Singer. Clarion Books, 2002. One frog, two owls, and three geese are joined by increasingly larger numbers of different animals that keep ten campers from falling asleep in their tents.

Raccoon on His Own by Jim Arnosky. Putnam, 2001. A curious young raccoon takes an unexpected trip downstream in a small wooden boat.

Raccoon Tune by Nancy Shaw. Henry Holt & Company, 2003. A family of raccoons prowl around a neighborhood making a ruckus until they find supper.

The Raft by Jim LaMarche. HarperCollins, 2000. Reluctant Nicky spends a wonderful summer with Grandma, who introduces him to the joy of rafting down the river near her home and watching the animals along the banks.

Sheep Take a Hike by Nancy Shaw. Houghton Mifflin, 1994. Having gotten lost on a chaotic hike in the great outdoors, the sheep find their way back by following the trail of wool they have left.

Splash in a Pond by Dana Meachen Rau. Rourke Press, 2001. Illustrations and brief text describe a visit to a pond, including clothes, equipment, and things to see and do.

Spruce the Moose Cuts Loose by Sarah Stapler. Putnam, 1992. Spruce the Moose's enormous antlers cause him all sorts of problems in his daily life.

Stella & Roy Go Camping by Ashley Wolff. Dutton Children's Books, 1999. During their camping trip, Roy continually tries to find evidence of bears in the animal tracks around them, only to be contradicted by his sister Stella, but then one night a bear really does appear.

Stella, Fairy of the Forest by Marie-Louise Gay. Groundwood Books, 2002. Stella and her little brother cross a field and a creek before spending the day in the forest. Butterflies, snakes, rocks, and sheep provide fuel for Sam's curious-little-brother questions and Stella's big-sister answers as they explore the outdoor world.

Turtle and Snake Go Camping by Kate Spohn. Puffin, 2000. Best friends Turtle and Snake go camping. They march around the tress and row across the pond until they find the perfect spot for their tent, but the dark woods are scary.

Walk in the Woods by Dana Meachen Rau. Rourke Press, 2001. A walk in the woods involves seeing tall trees and silly squirrels, collecting leaves, and listening for birds.

What Use Is a Moose? by Martin Waddell. Candlewick Press, 1996. When Jack's efforts to find a use for the moose he has brought home end in disaster, Jack's mother says the moose has to go—until she realizes that being loved is the best use of all.

When Daddy Took Us Camping by Julie Brillhart. Albert Whitman, 1997. A brother and sister share an exciting night camping with their father.

When the Fireflies Come by Jonathan London. Dutton Children's Books, 2003. Screen doors slam, hot dogs and burgers cook on the grill, and then there's baseball. But when the fireflies come out, it's time to chase them and catch them and then set them free to watch them dance and light up the night.

When We Go Camping by Margriet Ruurs. Tundra Books, 2001. An adventure in nature is described as children go camping. Painted illustrations add to the unique beauty of this book. The back has a legend with animal tracks and basic information on the animals you can find in each painting.

Where Once there Was a Wood by Denise Fleming. Henry Holt & Company, 2000. Examines the many forms of wildlife that can be displaced if their environment is destroyed by development, and discusses how communities and schools can provide spaces for animals to live.

Who Lives in the Pond? by Julie Aigner-Clark. Hyperion, 2003. Tadpole swims in the pond and points out all the different wildlife that live there, too.

Zigby Camps Out by Brian Paterson. HarperCollins, 2003. Zigby is going camping with his friends, Bertie and McMeer. But when they head into the deepest, darkest jungle, a night under the stars turns into an adventure they'll never forget!

Name Tag Patterns for The Great Outdoors

Name Tag Patterns for The Great Outdoors

Name Tag Patterns for The Great Outdoors